Hidden

HOLLAND

SASKIA NAAFS & GUIDO VAN EIJCK

T0348993

INTRODUCTION

Hidden Holland is an alternative travel guide filled with inspiring stories about more than 390 unique and unexpected places all around the Netherlands. This guide entreats you to leave the beaten path by pointing you to locations that many people don't even know about, like a forest full of miniature waterworks, a small Frisian church with a mummy in its cellar, and secret NATO headquarters.

This guide aims to stimulate your senses, arouse your curiosity and take you to places with a special story. Get inspired by a unique village that once served as a testing ground for modernist architects, or a museum full of bizarre inventions that were never built. Walk through a castle garden with 21(!) different kinds of landscapes or enjoy freshly made fries at a snack bar with a view on the entrance to Europe's biggest port.

The Netherlands is known for its windmills, tulip fields and picturesque villages, but there is so much more to visit, including spectacular stone quarries, exceptional private collections and lovely walled cities. What's more, the Netherlands boasts plenty of amazing museums, varied architecture and surprising natural areas.

This guide is anything but exhaustive. The best way to explore this fascinating country is to visit the local VVV tourist office or read up on a local website. The main idea behind *Hidden Holland* is to draw you away from the usual attractions and encourage you to visit the more unusual and lesser-known places. Some of these may be a little difficult to find or are only open a few days a month. Sometimes the address has changed or the place is (temporarily) closed. In that case, you will have to exercise patience – but you will always encounter something special when you venture out to explore the country.

ABOUT THE AUTHORS

Saskia Naafs and Guido van Eijck are writers and researchers from Rotterdam. While writing *Hidden Holland,* they drew on their own experiences, and those of their friends and family. They travelled up and down the country: to Zeeland and Southern Limburg, and from the tip of North-Holland via the Afsluitdijk to Friesland. They were pleasantly surprised by the hidden histories, the impressive architecture, the intriguing museums, the solemn statues, the myriads of cultural highlights, and the shops, pubs, restaurants and hotels that they encountered in all twelve provinces of the Netherlands. They are also the authors of the city guides on Amsterdam and Rotterdam in *The 500 Hidden Secrets* series.

HOW TO USE THIS BOOK

The idea behind this guide is that it lists the places that the authors would recommend to a good friend who is in search of a surprising destination or an unusual experience. It is different from other travel guides, in that places are listed by category, rather than by location. The maps help you find the various locations, so you can put together a trip that connects these different places with each other.

Most of the destinations in the guide can be reached by train, by bike and on foot. Now and then you'll need a car to get to more remote destinations. Where possible, the authors recommend you to use public transport. You can rent a bicycle almost everywhere and take your bike with you on the train.

One of the best ways to explore the Netherlands is by bike after all. The cycling routes and bicycle junctions are well indicated and there's always a nice pub or place to eat nearby. It only makes it easier to choose routes that wind their way along nice cycling trails, through city centres or quiet nature areas.

What's even more fun is to get around on foot because you always see more, than if you travel by bike or by car. The often centuries-old Dutch cities are designed to be admired at the leisurely human pace of 3 km/hour. So pop this guide in your bag, grab an umbrella, switch off your phone and head out on a mini adventure. It's the only way to discover the many strange and inspiring places in the Netherlands.

DISCOVER MORE ONLINE

Hidden Holland is part of the internationally successful travel guide series called *The 500 Hidden Secrets.* The series covers over 40 destinations and includes city guides, regional guides and guides that focus on a specific theme.

Curious about the other destinations? Or looking for inspiration for your next city trip? Visit THE500HIDDENSECRETS.COM. Here you can order every guide from our online shop and find tons of interesting travel content.

Also, don't forget to follow us on Instagram or Facebook for dreamy travel photos and ideas, as well as up-to-date information. Our socials are the easiest way to get in touch with us: we love hearing from you and appreciate all feedback.

the500hiddensecrets

@500hiddensecrets   #500hiddensecrets

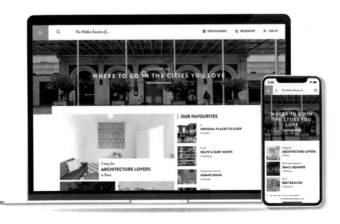

HOLLAND

1 GRONINGEN

2 FRIESLAND

3 DRENTHE

4 OVERIJSSEL

5 FLEVOLAND

6 NORTH HOLLAND

7 UTRECHT

8 GELDERLAND

9 SOUTH HOLLAND

10 ZEELAND

11 NORTH BRABANT

12 LIMBURG

1 GRONINGEN

Wadden Sea Area

Lauwersoog

Pieterburen

Usquert

Zeerijp

Delfzijl

Groningen

Slochteren

Nieuwe Statenzijl

Leek

Haren

Bad Nieuweschans

Bourtange

2 FRIESLAND

Wadden Sea Area

Schiermonnikoog

Ameland
(Hollum)

Terschelling
(Oosterend)

Vlieland

Tytsjerk

Franeker

Leeuwarden

Harlingen

Earnewâld

Kornwerderzand

Wiuwert

Drachten

Bolsward

Workum

Mildam

Sloten

Stavoren

Balk

Warns

Lemmer

3 DRENTHE

Veenhuizen

Assen

Drouwen

Hooghalen

Vledder
Frederiksoord

Ruinen

4 OVERIJSSEL

Weerribben-
Wieden
National Park

● Zwolle

Lattrop-
Breklenkamp
●
Ootmarsum ●
●
Denekamp
De Lutte
●
Ambt Delden
●
● Deventer
Enschede
●

5 FLEVOLAND

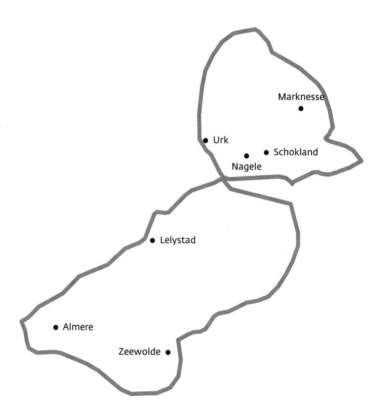

Marknesse •

• Urk

Nagele • • Schokland

Lelystad •

• Almere

Zeewolde •

6 NORTH HOLLAND

De Cocksdorp

Wadden Sea Area

Texel

Oudeschild

Huisduinen

Den Oever

Wieringen

Wieringerwerf

Callantsoog

Medemblik

Winkel

Schoorl

Enkhuizen

Bergen

Alkmaar

Graft

Wijk aan Zee

Zaandam

IJmuiden

Driehuis

Marken

Santpoort-Zuid

Bloemendaal

Ruigoord

Zandvoort

Haarlem

Amsterdam

Muiden

Naarden

Laren

Hilversum

7 UTRECHT

Vierhouten

Garderen

Gorssel

Kootwijk

Zutphen

Hoenderloo

Otterlo

Lunteren

De Hoge Veluwe
National Park

Dieren

Arnhem

Rheden

Doesb

Doorwerth

Rozendaal

Wageningen

Oosterbeek

Erichem

Kedichem

Hernen

Herwijnen

Poederoijen

Batenburg

Nijmegen

Ouddorp

Noordwijk

Katwijk aan
Zee
Rijnsburg • Oegstgeest
Wassenaar
Leiden

Scheveningen

Bodegraven

The Hague • Voorburg

Rijswijk
Delft

Hoek van
Holland

Everdingen

Rotterdam
Schiedam
Kinderdijk
Leerdam

ckanje
Rhoon

Dordrecht

10 ZEELAND

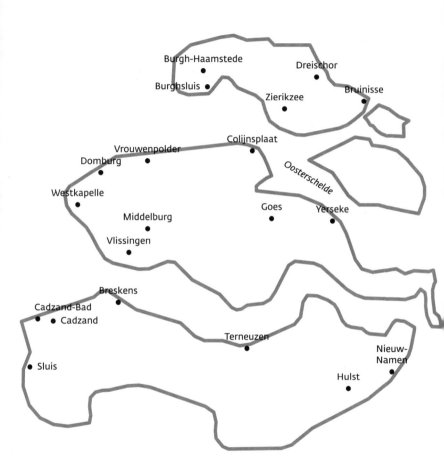

Burgh-Haamstede

Dreischor

Burghsluis

Bruinisse

Zierikzee

Colijnsplaat

Vrouwenpolder

Domburg

Oosterschelde

Westkapelle

Goes

Yerseke

Middelburg

Vlissingen

Breskens

Cadzand-Bad

Cadzand

Terneuzen

Nieuw-Namen

Sluis

Hulst

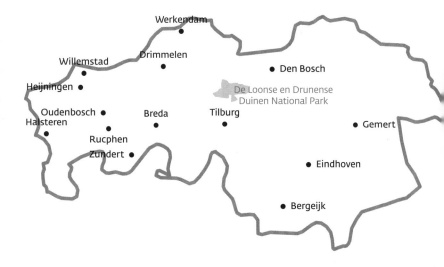

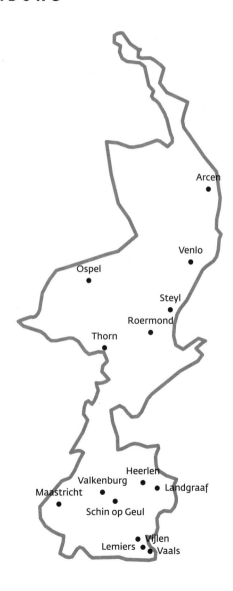

Arcen

Venlo

Ospel

Steyl

Roermond

Thorn

Heerlen

Valkenburg

Landgraaf

Maastricht

Schin op Geul

Vijlen

Lemiers

Vaals

LOVE – LEEUWARDEN

ART and CULTURE Ⓐ

STATUE

stories

---

1 **DELFT BLUE JESUS**
MUSEUM VAALS
Eschberg 7
Vaals
Limburg
+31 (0)43 306 00 80
museumvaals.nl

Jesus also moves with the times as you see at the entrance of the museum in Vaals. A caravan dweller from Landgraaf left without taking this 4,5-metre-tall statue of the Redeemer with him so it was given a second lease on life in Vaals. The famous graffiti and stencil artist Hugo Kaagman used Christian symbolism in Delft blue, adding a large 'S' to the pedestal. The museum has a collection of over 200 statues of saints.

2 **BUTT PLUG GNOME**
Eendrachtsplein
[Centre]
Rotterdam
South Holland

Wherever Paul McCarthy pops up, controversy inevitably follows. The Parisians were not enthused when they saw the rather suggestive shape of McCarthy's Christmas tree, which was installed near the Louvre. His statue of St. Nick for the city of Rotterdam also got people's knickers in a twist because instead of a Christmas tree Santa seems to be holding a butt plug. And that's how this statue got its nickname, the Butt Plug Gnome. The locals, however, objected to its installation. After several peregrinations it ended up here, after the Nieuwe Binnenweg traders' association lobbied, successfully, to have it installed in the square. The gnome has since become a popular Instagram feature and a place to meet.

4 STALIN IN A PHONE BOOTH

3 MANNES THE DOG

Stationsstraat
Assen
Drenthe

The installation of Mannes the dog at the entrance to the train station in Assen soon set tongues wagging. This six-metre-tall wood sculpture was deemed too expensive, too menacing and how on earth did it relate to Assen? A compromise was soon found, in typical Dutch fashion. The dog was repainted, from its original black into a friendlier brown and the TV screens in the dog's belly were cancelled. As the inauguration drew closer, the people of Assen gradually embraced Mannes. The sculpture was revealed on World Animal Day in 2018, which was renamed Mannes Day for the occasion. This loyal four-legged friend greets travellers as they set foot in the city.

4 STALIN IN A PHONE BOOTH

Eisenhouwerlaan,
Statenplein
bus stop
The Hague
South Holland

For 16 years, Stalin enjoyed a good view of the sex workers and their punters in Geleenstraat in The Hague from his boudoir-style phone booth. The 'man of steel' (his real name was Dzughashvili) loved women and herring, hence the fish in front of his nose and the location. The residents of Geleenstraat were not that happy with his presence however: they chucked stones at the Soviet dictator, used his phone booth as a public lavatory and a rubbish bin. In 2002, this artwork by Vitaly Komar and Alexander Melamid was therefore moved to a new location near the Photo Museum, with a view of the stately Statenkwartier. The question remains whether anyone still remembers that this is actually an anti-communist artwork.

5 EASTER ISLAND ON TEXEL

Postweg 72
Zuid-Eierland
De Cocksdorp
Texel
North Holland
+31 (0)222 31 12 14
eilandgalerij.nl

On 5 April 1722, Jacob Roggeveen and his crew were the first Europeans ever to set foot on Easter Island (Rapa Nui). Less than impressed by the barren island, the crew members from Texel decided to move on to Indonesia after a few days. 250 years later, the ties between the islands of Texel and Rapa Nui, which are similar in size, were strengthened when the artist Bene Aukara Tuki Pate spent two months on Texel carving this *Rapa Nui dreamer* out of stone. The Moai statue can be found in the garden of the Eiland Gallery, and faces Easter Island.

6 MAIGRET IN DELFZIJL

Intersection
Jaagpad/
Ringenum
Delfzijl
Groningen

Maigret looks somewhat out of sorts here in Delfzijl. The broad-shouldered, imposing inspector with his iconic fur collar and bowler hat, who was the subject of many of Simenon's books, actually looks rather small here. The field is mainly frequented by dog owners. In 1929, Georges Simenon stranded in Delfzijl with his boat, and was forced to spend a few days here. He soon fell in love with the tiny village and waited in the local pubs for his boat to be repaired. In his memoirs he wrote: "I had a few shots of *jenever,* and, feeling drowsy, I could make out a massive, imperturbable male figure, who, in my opinion, could be an acceptable commissioner. I spent the rest of the day adding objects to this figure: a pipe, a bowler hat, a heavy overcoat and a velvet collar." Maigret was the protagonist of 75 novels and 28 short stories. He even crossed the Atlantic Ocean but his adventures started here, in tiny Delfzijl.

Cities full of **STREET ART**

---

7 **HEERLEN
STREET ART**

Heerlen
Limburg
+31 (0)6 29 20 98 91
heerlenmurals.nl

The undisputed street art capital of the
Netherlands is Heerlen. At one time, this city, in
a former mining region, was the most prosperous
city in the South. Once the mines closed, people's
fortunes changed and the city suffered from
vacancy and dilapidation. And that is exactly the
kind of backdrop that graffiti artists love. In 2013,
the first works popped up and since then Heerlen
has been transformed into a large open-air street
art gallery with works by internationally renowned
artists. The local tourist office organises tours, but
you can also buy the *Street Art Heerlen* guide or map
your own route on the website listed above.

8 **MERWE-
VIERHAVEN
ROTTERDAM**

Keilewerf 1 and 2
[West]
Rotterdam
South Holland
rewriters010.nl

In the old days, this area between the port and the
railway tracks was a no man's land, a dodgy place
where you would mainly run into sex workers and
drug dealers. Nowadays, Keilewerf is home to hip
companies and internationally renowned artists such
as Joep van Lieshout and Daan Roosegaarde. In the
long term, the city also hopes to build housing here.
For the time being, however, you can admire the
works of several street artists on the large industrial
buildings. A lush community garden (a design by
LOLA Landscape Architects) makes this area all the
more special.

9 KEITH HARING IN AMSTERDAM

Willem de Zwijgerlaan/ Jan van Galenstraat [West] Amsterdam North Holland

When world-famous pop art artist Keith Haring had his first solo exhibition in Amsterdam's Stedelijk Museum in 1986, he made a site-specific work for everyone to enjoy. His canvas: a 40-foot wall outside the museum's storage facility. The building became an indoor market and for 30-odd years, this huge mural of a dog with a fish tail was concealed under a thick steel plate. Following the redevelopment of this neighbourhood, 'the Haring' reappeared. You can see the top of the mural when you turn onto Willem de Zwijgerlaan from Jan van Galenstraat. You'll have to enter the Food Center site if you want to see the entire mural.

7 HEERLEN STREET ART

10 GOES STREET ART

Goes
Zeeland
goesisgoes.nl/
muralgoes

Most people would not associate the provincial city of Goes with street art but there's no getting around it. The centre is filled with the most fantastic and colourful creations. In 2015, the city hosted a major street art festival, called Mural Goes, which resulted in 11 large works and since then, they have added many more.

11 EINDHOVEN STREET ART

Eindhoven
North Brabant
eindhoven.street
artcities.com

Eindhoven has transformed itself into one of the most lively and exciting cities in Brabant in a relatively short time. And this means it also has plenty of street art. Head to the famous Dommel Tunnel next to the city's Central Station, where you can see Monthy Python's *Ministry of Silly Walks*, which was inaugurated by John Cleese himself in 2016. The Berenkuil (Bear pit, Insulindeplein) is an official graffiti site, where you can see lots of works, that change often. There are also some gigantic murals near Strijp-S and the PSV Stadium.

11 EINDHOVEN STREET ART

Picturesque
ARTISTS' VILLAGES

12 **BERGEN**
North Holland

The first artists moved to Bergen around 1900. The sea, the dunes, the panoramic views and the amazing light were preferred subjects, as were the characteristic buildings in the village such as the ruined church and the town hall. Bergen even had its own art movement, called the Bergen School, a precursor of Dutch Expressionism. Head to Kranenburgh Museum to find out more about it. Charley Toorop lived and worked here, and Piet Mondrian, Gerrit Rietveld and Pyke Koch all visited the village between the dunes and the forest. Bergen still has an artistic feel to it. Poets and writers often stay in the former home of the poet Adriaan Roland Holst as artists in residence and there are also plenty of galleries to discover here.

13 **DOMBURG**
Zeeland

Domburg is another example of artists preferring to live by the sea. Many generations of elegant Dutch families spent their holiday in this upmarket, stylish seaside resort, which also attracted many artists in the early 20th century, including Piet Mondrian. The grandeur of this seaside tourism is especially obvious in the Bathing Pavilion, which dates from 1889. It has since been transformed into a restaurant, where you can enjoy lunch, dinner or a drink. The Marie Tak van Poortvliet Museum has its own collection of works which are related to Domburg.

14 LAREN
North Holland

Anton Mauve (1838-1888), one of the founders of the Laren School, who is also regarded as a follower of the Hague School, painted the most beautiful paintings of the region around Laren. His canvases of sweeping heaths, flocks of sheep and lonely shepherds are simply unrivalled. He lived opposite the Singer Laren Museum, which has a good visual arts collection, from 1880 to 1950. Mauve married one of Vincent van Gogh's cousins and Vincent even briefly apprenticed with him.

15 OOTMARSUM
Overijssel

Ootmarsum calls itself 'the art city of the east'. It is situated in the picturesque landscape of Twente, near the lovely Dinkel River. Ootmarsum has an old town centre, with plenty of half-timbered buildings and galleries. One of the most famous artists to live in this village is painter Ton Schulten, who has his own museum (and shop) in the eponymous square.

16 RUIGOORD
North Holland

One of the last real safe havens of Amsterdam, where the hippy atmosphere of the sixties still lingers. The abandoned village was squatted in the early seventies and since then Ruigoord is occupied by artists, even though its existence is perennially under threat due to the port's expansion. There are plenty of open studio weekends, markets and festivals here. The best-known festival is the annual Landjuweel festival, which is organised every summer.

DESIGN HEROES:
from De Stijl to Dutch Design

---

17 RIETVELD SCHRÖDER HOUSE
Prins Hendrik-laan 50-A
Utrecht
rietveldschroderhuis.nl

Truus Schröder-Schräder spent 60 years of her life in this villa, which was built for her by Gerrit Rietveld, the artist, furniture builder and architect of De Stijl. It was his first design for a complete house. After her death in 1985, the villa was restored. It is now managed by the Centraal Museum, which has the world's largest Rietveld collection. You can take a guided tour of the house and also see some of Rietveld's most famous furniture designs here.

18 DIRK VAN DER KOOIJ
Kanonnenloods 24
Zaandam
North Holland
+31 (0)20 247 96 00
dirkvanderkooij.com

Dirk van der Kooij is famous for his 3D printed chairs made of residual plastic. You can find his chubby chairs in several museum collections and the Dutch king Willem Alexander even owns a few. Van der Kooij studied at the Design Academy in Eindhoven. In 2014, he opened a studio in Hembrugterrein in Zaandam. In addition to designing chairs, van der Kooij also produces planters, vases, speakers and luminaires, all made from residual materials.

17 RIETVELD SCHRÖDER HOUSE

19 PIET HEIN EEK

**Halvemaan-
straat 30
Eindhoven
North Brabant
+31 (0)40 285 66 10**
pietheineek.nl

It all started with a reclaimed wood cabinet, which Piet Hein Eek designed while he was still studying at the Design Academy in Eindhoven. Since then he has become one of the Netherlands' most famous designers. He even collaborated with IKEA. In 2010, Eek moved back to Eindhoven, where he set up shop on the site of the former Philips plant, called Strijp-R (not to be confused with Strijp-S). Here he has now created his own version of Piet Hein Eek heaven, complete with a large shop, showroom, events space and restaurant.

19 PIET HEIN EEK

20 SONNEVELD HOUSE

20 SONNEVELD HOUSE

Jongkindstraat 12
[Centre]
Rotterdam
South Holland
+31 (0)10 440 12 00
huissonneveld.nl

This villa near Rotterdam's Museum Park is the best-preserved example of a house in the New Building (Nieuwe Bouwen) style, which promoted a pragmatic approach to buildings, with straight lines, and plenty of light, air and space. Brinkman and Van der Vlugt, who designed the Van Nelle factory and Feyenoord Stadium, built this house for the Sonneveld family in the thirties. The house is full of Gispen furniture and is a representative example of a house of a prominent family in Rotterdam during this era. The colours of the interior design scheme were inspired by Bart van der Leck, a painter who belonged to the De Stijl movement.

21 ANDAZ HOTEL

Prinsengracht 587
[Centre]
Amsterdam
North Holland
+31 (0)20 523 12 34
hyatt.com

Marcel Wanders is one of the Dutch Design stars, and is famous for his unique, exuberant style. As you walk past the Andaz Hotel on Prinsengracht, you will inevitably be drawn to the baroque interior with its many references to Holland's glorious past, from the Golden Age to Delft blue, tulips, clogs and even Johan Cruijff. You can enjoy a drink in the lobby or spend the night here. Wanders designed all the rooms of this five-star hotel. Are you a real Wanders fan and do you want to take home one of his designs? Then visit his shop, called Moooi, at Westerstraat 187.

21 ANDAZ HOTEL

Inspiring
ARTISTS' HOUSES

22 VILLA MONDRIAAN
Zonnebrink 4
Winterswijk
Gelderland
+31 (0)543 51 54 00
villamondriaan.nl

Art historians say that you can recognise the apple tree that Piet Mondrian painted from his parents' house in Winterswijk, in every artwork he produced, including his increasingly abstract work. He lived here from the age of eight and left when he was twenty. The house has been beautifully renovated and showcases several early works by this groundbreaking artist. The museum also hosts temporary exhibitions and has a nice collection of photos of Mondrian in Paris. There's also an apple tree in the garden again.

23 VINCENT VAN GOGH HOUSE
Markt 26-27
Zundert
North Brabant
+31 (0)76 597 85 90
vangoghhuis.com

Vincent van Gogh was born in this verger's house in Zundert, where he lived until the age of 16. You can find out more about Van Gogh's childhood and teenage years here. His father was the minister of the church next to the house. You can also find the grave of his brother, who was also called Vincent and was stillborn, one year before Vincent's birth. The Vincent van Gogh House has an audio tour and hosts interesting temporary exhibitions. It also showcases the works of the artists in residence, who stay in the atelier next to the house, and are inspired by Van Gogh.

24 MUSEUM TROMP'S HUYS

Dorpsstraat 99
Vlieland
Friesland
+31 (0)562 45 16 00
trompshuys.nl

Betzy Akersloot-Berg was an emancipated woman and a 19th-century adventurer. She was raised in Norway and worked as a nurse with the Sami. At the age of 30, she left for Munich, to become an apprentice of the artist Otto Sinding. Four years later, she departed for Scheveningen, where she studied with painter H.W. Mesdag. Even when she had settled on Vlieland with her husband, she continued to travel and paint a lot, in the style of the Hague School. You can see many of her works in her old home, called Tromp's Huys, which is also the oldest house on Vlieland. The salon looks just like it did in 1900, when the dignitaries of Vlieland met here for a chat.

25 STUDIO DICK BRUNA

CENTRAAL MUSEUM
Agnietenstraat 1
Utrecht
centraalmuseum.nl

He will forever be associated with the white bunny Miffy but Dick Bruna created many other characters, including hundreds of book covers for the De Zwarte Beertjes publishing house. He was able to infuse his pared-down, minimalist designs with plenty of expression. Dick Bruna also said that he was influenced by the De Stijl art movement. He was one of Utrecht's most famous residents, which is why, upon his death, his study in the attic of his home in the city centre was moved to the attic of the Central Museum. The archivists catalogued everything in it, such as his books, crayons, typewriter and letters from Japanese fans.

26 CUYPERS HOUSE

**Pierre Cuypers-
straat 1
Roermond
Limburg
+31 (0)475 35 91 02**
*cuypershuis
roermond.nl*

Pierre Cuypers lived in the Cuypers House, which he also designed himself. Roermond's most famous son left his mark on the Netherlands as an architect, designing two of Amsterdam's most iconic buildings, Central Station and the Rijksmuseum, as well as the lavishly decorated De Haar Castle in Utrecht. He also designed or restored countless churches and castles. Cuypers adored the neo-Gothic style and an elaborate decor. The museum focusses on his crafstmanship, as well as featuring contemporary artists.

27 REMBRANDT HOUSE

**Jodenbreestraat 4
[Centre]
Amsterdam
North Holland
+31 (0)20 520 04 00**
rembrandthuis.nl

Rembrandt van Rijn bought this stately house in Amsterdam in the same year he received the commission for his famous *The Night Watch*. In 1639, real estate was just as expensive in the city as it is now. Ultimately the steep mortgage payments forced him to declare bankruptcy. Nevertheless, Rembrandt spent 20 very productive years here. The museum features 17th-century furniture and has a sizeable collection of Rembrandt's engravings.

Fascinating
CLASSICS COLLECTIONS

28 **TEYLERS MUSEUM**
Spaarne 16
Haarlem
North Holland
+31 (0)23 516 09 60
teylersmuseum.nl

Since its opening in 1784, Teylers, the oldest museum in the Netherlands, has been a place where art and science go hand in hand. It was a knowledge institution where people could explore the world without any guidance from the church or state. Whereas many science and natural history museums have since gone interactive, Teylers still exudes the appetite for knowledge of times past. Here you can see antique scientific instruments and display cases full of minerals and fossils, including the 150-million-year-old bird-like dinosaur, called the Archaeopteryx. The art collection features prints by Michelangelo and Raphael and paintings from the Dutch romantic period.

29 **FRANS HALS MUSEUM**
Groot Heilig-land 62
Haarlem
North Holland
+31 (0)23 511 57 75
franshalsmuseum.nl

Frans Hals influenced Impressionists such as Monet and Van Gogh with his lively portraits of the 17th-century elite and the lower classes many centuries after his death. Nobody used the colour black with quite as much depth as Hals. You can see a dozen works by this artist in Haarlem, the city where he spent most of his life. The ticket also serves as your admission to the Hal (Grote Markt 16), where you can see the city's modern art collection.

30 THE MESDAG COLLECTIE

**Laan van
Meerdervoort 7-F
The Hague
South Holland
+31 (0)70 362 14 34
*demesdagcollectie.nl***

While a career switch at the age of 35 is the norm rather than the exception these days, it was considered quite remarkable at the time when Hendrik and Sientje Mesdag decided to become painters. Mesdag is famous for his seascapes and the Mesdag Panorama, which Sientje helped paint. She painted landscapes and still lifes. The couple also acquired a fabulous art collection during their lifetime, which they opened to the public. Nowadays you can see works here by the painters of the Hague School (like Jozef Israëls, Willem Maris) and French painters of the Barbizon School (including Roussau and Millet) and many other artworks, in the 19th-century home of the Mesdags.

31 THE MAURITSHUIS

**Plein 29
The Hague
South Holland
+31 (0)70 302 34 56
*mauritshuis.nl***

The collection of the Mauritshuis is exhibited on two floors of a 17th-century dwelling next to the Binnenhof. In a sense, it's the little brother of the Rijksmuseum in Amsterdam: it's significantly smaller but the works are of superb quality. The emphasis is on Dutch Masters of the Golden Age and works include Fabritius's *The Goldfinch*, Rembrandt's *The Anatomy Lesson of Dr. Nicolaes Tulp* and Paulus Potter's *The Bull*. And don't get us started on Hans Holbein's magnificent portraits and the only work of Rogier van der Weyden in the Netherlands.

32 **WERELDMUSEUM**
Willemskade 25
[Centre]
Rotterdam
South Holland
+31 (0)10 270 71 72
wereldmuseum.nl

The Wereldmuseum is the outcome of two centuries of collecting in a port city. The Royal Dutch Yacht Club used to be located here in the 1850s. Many of its members regularly donated items from around the world. In 1883, the resulting museum was transferred to the municipality, which decided to establish an ethnographic museum here. The collection includes masterpieces from Africa, Asia and Oceania, including a Congolese nail fetish and Buddhist religious art.

33 UNIVERSITY MUSEUM

**Oude Kijk in
't Jatstraat 7-A
Groningen
+31 (0)50 363 50 83
rug.nl/museum**

Groningen's University Museum showcases highlights of 400 years of university history, in a classic first floor hall with glass display cases. They include an orangutan head in a jar, which led to a real 'orangutan war', and the first electric car from 1835, as well as an Egyptian mummy and an early X-ray from 1896. There is also a separate anatomy room, with foetuses in jars and 18th-century tattoos. You can also find the consultation room of Aletta Jacobs here. This doctor and feminist was the first woman in the Netherlands to obtain a university degree.

Completely
UNIQUE COLLECTIONS

34 BIZARIUM

Hoogstraat 35
Sluis
Zeeland
+31 (0)117 85 28 08
bizarium.com

"A tribute to all the inventors of yore, and a call to today's creative thinkers", says the inscription at the entrance of this unique museum in Sluis, Zeeland. The Bizarium is the constantly growing collection of inventions that were never built. The Flemish designers Marc De Jonghe and Ann Geerinck built all of them themselves, drawing on patent drawings, engravings and other historical sources. You can see Leonardo da Vinci's self-driving car here, made from wooden cogs, hinges and pins. And if you're fortunate, you will even be given a demo. We can't reveal any more than this and it's worth noting that the museum has a strict no photos policy. The audio tours, which infuse these discoveries with a certain literary quality, are highly recommended. You will leave the museum surprised and delighted at such ingenuity and optimism.

35 DEAD ANIMALS WITH A BACKSTORY

MUSEUM OF
NATURAL HISTORY
Westzeedijk 345
[Centre]
Rotterdam
South Holland
+31 (0)10 436 42 22
hetnatuurhistorisch.nl

The hedgehog that was killed by a McFlurry cup, the weasel who stopped the Large Hadron Collider at CERN and the house sparrow that almost spoiled 'Domino Day 2005'. The Museum of Natural History in Rotterdam has a display case full of 'dead animals with a backstory', which were collected by Kees Moeliker, one of the most prominent biologists in the Netherlands, who is also the museum's director.

36 CAT MUSEUM

Herengracht 497
[Centre]
Amsterdam
North Holland
+31 (0)20 626 90 40
kattenkabinet.nl

In loving memory of his ginger cat John Pierpont Morgan, Bob Meijer decided to transform his 17th-century town house on the canals into a museum of cat art. JP is prominently featured in some of the paintings, but the collection in itself is also quite unique, with canvases by artists like Henri de Toulouse-Lautrec, Tsuguharu Foujita, Pablo Picasso and Théophile Steinlen. And did you ever imagine that you would come across a portrait of Lenin with a cat draped over his arm? Don't trip over the live cats who skulk through the rooms.

37 MUSEUM VROLIK
ACADEMIC
MEDICAL CENTRE
**Building Jo –
Room 130
Meibergdreef 15
[Southeast]
Amsterdam
North Holland
+31 (0)20 566 49 27**
museumvrolik.nl

In the 18th, 19th and 20th centuries, Amsterdam scientists compiled a collection of study materials for an anatomical laboratory. The result is a fascinating and sometimes slightly eerie collection, including an open head in a jar, with the brain protruding, the eye of a whale and the tattooed skin of a sailor. The exhibition can be found in the medical faculty of the Academic Medical Centre (Building J, Room 130) in the southeast of the city.

35 **MUSEUM OF NATURAL HISTORY**

38 DE LIBRIJE CHAIN LIBRARY

ST. WALBURGA'S
CHURCH
Kerkhof 3
Zutphen
Gelderland
+31 (0)575 54 70 58
librije-zutphen.nl

The 741 books in the library of St. Walburga's Church are all chained to the shelves so they cannot be taken from the De Librije reading room. This chain library dates from the 1560s and is the only such library in the Netherlands. Council members and preachers would read the right books here, the kind of literature that would not undermine their 'true' faith. The 16th-century collection is still complete and is still largely in its original state. Don't forget to admire the floor tiles, which feature legs here and there. They are said to be the devil's.

39 JAPAN MUSEUM SIEBOLD HOUSE

Rapenburg 19
Leiden
South Holland
+31 (0)71 512 55 39
sieboldhuis.org

In the 1820s, Philipp Franz von Siebold was a GP in the trading post of Deshima, an island off the coast of Nagasaki from where Dutch merchants were the only westerners to have access to Japan for several decades. After two maps of Japan were found in his house, he was expelled from the country for suspected espionage, and decided to move back to Leiden. His former home has now been transformed into the Japan Museum. In addition to temporary exhibitions, you can also see the large collection of prints, fossils, and other treasures that Von Siebold brought back from Japan.

40 NATIONAL GLASS MUSEUM

Lingedijk 28-30
Leerdam
South Holland
+31 (0)345 61 49 60
nationaal glasmuseum.nl

In the early 20th century, P.M. Cochius ran the Glasfabriek Leerdam, inviting such artists as Berlage and Copier to design glassware that looked interesting but was still affordable. Soon the small town of Leerdam became synonymous with unique glassware. The National Glass Museum, which opened its doors in 1953, has a permanent glass collection from Leerdam and beyond.

Museums for
CONTEMPORARY ART

41 **MUSEUM VOORLINDEN**
Buurtweg 90
Wassenaar
South Holland
+31 (0)70 512 16 60
voorlinden.nl

Contemporary art is sometimes perceived as inaccessible and alienating. But the art in Museum Voorlinden encourages you to move closer or even become part of it. Take Leandro Erlich's swimming pool: you can see the museum gallery above you from the bottom of the pool through the water. Or the seemingly endless journey through Richard Serra's heavy metal structure. As you bend your knees to take a closer look at Maurizio Cattelan's mini lifts, you feel like Alice in Wonderland. The collector Joop van Caldenborgh built this museum to share his enormous art collection with the public. The sleek new build and the lavish Voorlinden country estate, in the dunes to the north of The Hague, blend into something new, which looks like it has always been there.

42 **DE PONT**
Wilhelminapark 1
Tilburg
North Brabant
+31 (0)13 543 83 00
depont.nl

When De Pont opened its doors in 1992 in a renovated spinning mill, using industrial heritage as a unique and prominent exhibition space was still unheard of. The museum is home to the art collection of entrepreneur Jan de Pont and is considered one of the best for contemporary art in the Netherlands. Its permanent collection includes works by Gerhard Richter, Marlene Dumas and Anish Kapoor, among others.

41 MUSEUM VOORLINDEN

42 DE PONT

43 VAN ABBEMUSEUM

Stratumsedijk 2
Eindhoven
North Brabant
+31 (0)40 238 10 00
vanabbemuseum.nl

In the mid-thirties, the cigar manufacturer Henri van Abbe wanted the people of Eindhoven to also be able to enjoy contemporary art, which is why he sponsored a new museum. The Van Abbemuseum only became famous after the war, transforming into one of the leading Dutch museums for modern art, following the acquisition of 20th-and 21th-century works. Highlights include works by the Russian constructivist El Lissitzky, making this one of the world's largest Lissitzky collections.

44 SCHUNCK*

Bongerd 18
Heerlen
Limburg
+31 (0)45 577 22 00
schunck.nl

The heavy doors, the visible reinforced concrete structure and the large windows. It is easy to see how the Schunck department store, built in 1936, got its nickname, the Glass Palace. The building is an international icon of the functionalist style in architecture and was built at a time when Heerlen was a prosperous city thanks to the mining industry. The building became rundown in the nineties and at one point its demolition was even on the cards. Fortunately it was renovated, after a design by the architects Jo Coenen and Wiel Arets. Nowadays SCHUNCK* is home to a library, a cinema, an architecture museum and a tavern with an amazing rooftop terrace on the fifth floor. The museum has its own collection of post-war Dutch works and often hosts surprising temporary exhibition with contemporary Dutch and international artists.

45 **NEST**
DCR
De Constant
Rebecqueplein 20-B
The Hague
South Holland
+31 (0)70 365 31 86
nestruimte.nl

The Nest art space hosts interesting contemporary art exhibitions year-round. It's a space to experiment, think and get inspired by other artists and art lovers from the Netherlands and beyond. The expansive art space is situated in the DCR, a cultural breeding ground in the monumental Hague Electricity Factory – the city's electricity is still produced in the adjoining hall. Dozens of artists and designers have their studios here.

Surprising ART MUSEUMS

**46 STEDELIJK
MUSEUM
SCHIEDAM**
Hoogstraat 112
Schiedam
South Holland
+31 (0)10 246 36 66
stedelijkmuseum-
schiedam.nl

The Stedelijk Museum Schiedam has a large collection of post-war art. The Cobra movement (with works by such artists as Karel Appel, Corneille and Constant) and the serial movement from after the sixties (with Jan Schoonhoven and Peter Struycken) are especially well-represented. It's not far from Rotterdam either, as Schiedam is a stop on the city's metro network.

**47 MUSEUM
VAN DE GEEST |
OUTSIDER ART**
Amstel 51
[Centre]
Amsterdam
North Holland
+31 (0)23 541 06 70
museum
vandegeest.nl

Art brut, autodidactic art, outsider art: in the past century, all these terms have been used to refer to the art of people on the fringe, away from the mainstream or suffering from various mental disorders. Amsterdam's Museum van de Geest | Outsider Art shines a spotlight on this art form. A collaboration between Het Dolhuys, the psychiatry museum in Haarlem, and the Hermitage Amsterdam, where the museum is located.

48 MUSEUM DR8888

Museumplein 2
Drachten
Friesland
+31 (0)512 51 56 47
museumdrachten.nl

Brothers Thijs and Evert Rinsema brought Dada to Drachten in Friesland. They were shoemakers and 'part-time' artists and poets. You can see their work in museum Dr8888, alongside works by Kurt Schwitters, Man Ray, Theo van Doesburg and Northern Dutch works from the period in between the two World Wars and the post-war period. You can also visit a museum house that Van Doesburg designed in 1921, according to the rules of De Stijl. It's like stepping into a life-size painting.

49 HUIS MARSEILLE, MUSEUM FOR PHOTOGRAPHY

Keizersgracht 401
[Centre]
Amsterdam
North Holland
+31 (0)20 531 89 89
huismarseille.nl

Huis Marseille regularly organises unique photo exhibitions in two stately town houses along Amsterdam's Keizersgracht. Unfortunately people tend to overlook it in favour of its more famous big brother, the FOAM. The exhibitions are selected for their artistic quality, in the widest possible sense and include documentary works as well as conceptual photography.

50 MUSEUM MORE

Hoofdstraat 28
Gorssel
Gelderland
+31 (0)575 76 03 00
museummore.nl

Collectors Hans and Monique Melchers had to build two museums to house their private collection of modern realist art. The lion's share can be found in the former town hall of Gorssel in Gelderland and features works by Dutch artists such as Charley Toorop and Pyke Koch. The beautifully renovated Ruurlo Castle (Vordenseweg 2, in Ruurlo) has a lot of work by Carel Willink, who caused a furore before and after World War II with his magical realistic style.

51 DE FUNDATIE

Blijmarkt 20
Zwolle
Overijssel
+31 (0)572 38 81 88
museumdefundatie.nl

The striking oval sphere on the rooftop of the former Law Courts does not in any way match with the rest of this 19th-century building. Inside, there is an exhibition space. It is the most recent addition to the De Fundatie Museum, which has earned quite a reputation in recent years for organising unique modern and contemporary art exhibitions.

52 KRÖLLER-MÜLLER MUSEUM

Houtkampweg 6
Otterlo
Gelderland
+31 (0)318 59 12 41
krollermuller.nl

Location, location, location… and this is possibly the best location ever for a museum as the Kröller-Müller Museum is situated in the Hoge Veluwe NP, with plenty of space for a 25-acre sculpture garden. The museum originated from the collection of Helene Kröller-Müller, who acquired just under 11.500 artworks in the early decades of the 20th century, together with her son. The collection includes 90 paintings and 180 drawings by Vincent van Gogh, whom they helped make famous.

51 DE FUNDATIE

ART *in unexpected places*

53 THE UFO ON THE INKWELL

Moreelsepark 3
Utrecht

In 1999, this strange, extraterrestrial object landed on the headquarters of railway manager ProRail. The artwork was part of the Panorama 2000 art event. Standing on the city's Dom church, you could see artworks all over the city. The UFO was designed by sculptor Marc Ruygrok and stands atop the largest brick building in the Netherlands, which is called the Inkwell or Inktpot. Most of the artworks of Panorama 2000 have since disappeared, but the UFO was allowed to remain in place after ProRail purchased it.

53 THE UFO ON THE INKWELL

54 **SEA LEVEL**
De Verbeelding 25
Zeewolde
Flevoland

This artwork by the American artist Richard Serra, which is his largest in Europe, consists of two concrete walls, measuring 200 metres each. They flank the canal. One of the walls is as tall as a dike, the other one is the same height as the sea level. Without the dike, the water would flood the landscape here, right up to the top of the artwork. When you walk past the wall, you feel as if you are briefly submerged only to emerge above the sea level again.

55 **LOVE**
Stationsplein
Leeuwarden
Friesland

When the government announced that international artists would be selected to design the 11 fountains in the Frisian Eleven Cities for Leeuwarden Cultural Capital 2018, the people were rather sceptical. Couldn't they have just given the job to some local artists? But these two children's heads by the Spanish sculptor Jaume Plensa soon stole everyone's hearts. You can see the fog that Plensa admired above the Frisian pastures at the foot of the heads.

56 **THE GREEN CATHEDRAL**
Waterlandseweg
Almere
Flevoland

The Cathedral of Reims, in the form of 178 'Lombardy poplars'. The people of Almere called this 'gothic cultivation project', as artist Marinus Boezem called it, *the Green Cathedral*. The same cathedral shape has been 'carved' out of the forest in the field alongside it. According to Boezem, a cathedral is the 'epitome of human skill', just like the Flevoland polders in the former Zuiderzee.

57 **ROTATING HOUSE**

57 ROTATING HOUSE

Hasselt
roundabout
Tilburg
North Brabant

According to the rotondological society (yes, it really does exist), John Körmeling's rotating house is one of the most successful examples of roundabout art in the Netherlands. According to the society, roundabout art should take into account the roundabout's round shape, must be easy to understand for random passers-by, and the design must be easy to read. Körmeling's open house is unambiguous and easy to distinguish. The house slowly turns on its axis. Nonetheless, this artwork, like so much other art in public space, was criticised as excessive expenditure by the town. It was even briefly squatted for this reason in 2009.

58 BIG FUNNEL MAN

A27 near the
Breda exit
Breda
North Brabant

Many of the people of Breda think that the man who lays here on the side of the road with a funnel in his mouth is just very thirsty after an evening on the tiles. In reality, artist Joep van Lieshout thought that the many commuters who spend hours in traffic here would perhaps recognise themselves in the reclining man, who looks as if he is being force-fed.

59 BOSPOLDER FOX

Schiedamseweg 280
[West]
Rotterdam
South Holland

Every now and then, a fox pops up in busy Rotterdam. These courageous and streetwise adventurers are a symbol of nature making its way into the city, says artist Florentijn Hofman. As a tribute to them, he designed a 25-metre-high fox that overlooks the busy and multicultural Schiedamseweg, in the Bospolder neighbourhood. The animal has a huge plastic bag in its mouth, referring to the market on nearby Grote Visserijplein and the many plastic bags that lie around after a market day.

Mysterious **MUMMIES**

---

60 **THE MUMMY CELLAR**

NICOLAS CHURCH
Terp 1
Wiuwert
Friesland
+31 (0)58 250 17 78
mummiekelder.nl

The religious Labadist sect spent some time in Wiuwert at the end of the 17th century. Are they in any way responsible for the contents of the crypt in the Nicolas church? In 1765, carpenters found 11 mummies here, four of which are still here. The bodies were extremely well preserved. It is still not quite clear why this natural mummification process is so successful here. The mummified cat and birds, which prove that a completely unique process takes place in this crypt, are more recent. Open from April to October, the church offers guided tours that really make the mummies come to life through their stories.

61 **THE MUMMY OF THE WHITE VILLAGE**

ST. MICHAEL'S CHURCH
Kerkberg 2
Thorn
Limburg
+31 (0)6 57 76 29 46

The cap on his head is somewhat at an angle, which only serves to accentuate the hollow eyes below it. This naturally mummified body was found in the early 20th century in St. Michael's Church in the white village of Thorn, which is very popular with tourists. The body was naked, but was clad in a priest's robe, to avoid shocking visitors. In 2006, research by the Academic Medical Centre in Amsterdam resolved that the man must have died in the early 17th century at the ripe old age of 75. The research also disproved a myth, namely that the mummified arm, in the crypt, is not St. Benedict's, as was assumed for many centuries.

62 EGYPTIAN MUMMY

ZEEUWS MUSEUM
Abdij (Plein)
Middelburg
Zeeland
+31 (0)118 65 30 00
zeeuwsmuseum.nl

The Egyptian mummy of a child from circa 330 BC is part of the really interesting cabinet of curiosities in the attic of this regional museum. The child was found alongside a mummified cat. You can see a series of objects from the colonies, in thematic order, in three large ship's chests, including a ship's clock from the silver fleet of Dutch naval hero Piet Heyn. The rest of the museum is equally surprising, thanks to the exciting and contemporary layout. Take the time to admire the unique collection of tapestries, depicting naval battles from the war with Spain.

62 EGYPTIAN MUMMY

63 THE YDE GIRL

DRENTS MUSEUM
Brink 1
Assen
Drenthe
+31 (0)592 37 77 73
drentsmuseum.nl

In 1897, two turf cutters found the leathery, naturally mummified body of a 16-year old girl in a peat bog in the fens around Drenthe. She must have died a violent death somewhere between 54 BC and 128 AD – she still has a rope around her neck and was stabbed. There are plenty of other bog bodies in the Drents Museum in Assen. In recent years, the museum has also hosted numerous surprising exhibitions on North Korean propaganda art, the Dead Sea Scrolls and the Terracotta Army of Xi'an, among others.

64 SENSAOS

RIJKSMUSEUM
VAN OUDHEDEN
Rapenburg 28
Leiden
South Holland
+31 (0)71 516 31 63
rmo.nl

This is the only Dutch museum to have such an extensive collection of ancient Egyptian artefacts. It includes mummies, sarcophagi, grave goods and even an entire temple in the entrance hall. The 16-year old girl Sensaos was born into a wealthy family and was embalmed and mummified in 109 AD. She was the first mummy in the Netherlands, at the end of the 1980s, whose face was reconstructed using a CT scan.

65 HUMAN AND ANIMAL MUMMIES

ALLARD PIERSON
MUSEUM
Oude Turfmarkt 127
[Centre]
Amsterdam
North Holland
+31 (0)20 525 55 01
allardpierson.nl

The Allard Pierson is somewhat overshadowed by the other museums in Amsterdam's city centre. This archaeological museum of the University of Amsterdam has a collection which focussed on ancient Egypt, Greece and the Roman Empire. It is the result of the collections of several professors who lectured at the university. You can see stunning sarcophagi, mummy portraits, an Egyptian mummy, a mummified scarab and even a mummified falcon here.

WESTERBORK CAMP

HISTORY ⬤

Fun **MONSTERS**?
Monstrous fun?

---

66 THE NOTHOSAURUS OF WINTERSWIJK

DE MUSEUMFABRIEK
Het Rozendaal 11
Enschede
Overijssel
+31 (0)53 201 20 99
demuseumfabriek.nl

The stone quarry at Winterswijk has yielded plenty of interesting discoveries in chalkstone layers dating from the Triassic period, when Winterswijk was still close to the sea. A giant jellyfish for example, as well as an extremely rare beetle and dinosaur bones and skulls. The Nothosaurus was a swimming dinosaur, with razor-sharp teeth and is also called the sea monster of Winterswijk. Its bones and skulls are kept in the depot of the Museumfabriek, where you can see plenty of other fossils that were unearthed in the quarry. Don't forget to look at the couple of Nothosaurus, that was created by Remie Bakker.

67 THE SEA MONSTER OF SCHEVENINGEN

MUZEE SCHEVENINGEN
Neptunus-
straat 90-92
The Hague
South Holland
+31 (0)70 350 08 30
*muzee
scheveningen.nl*

This tiny creature couldn't be more different from Disney's 'Little Mermaid'. It looks like it belongs in a horror movie more than anything else. A monkey's body has been attached to a fish tail, possibly by a creative Japanese or Chinese fisherman, who used to sell these 'mermaids' for plenty of cash to American and European collectors with wunderkammers. These creative forgeries even had their own scientific name, namely pseudosiren paradoxoides.

68 THE FISH FOR STAVOREN

Stationsweg 1
(square)
Stavoren
Friesland

When it became known that an Amsterdam curator was going to use European funds to invite international artists to design 11 fountains for the 11 Frisian cities, the locals were less than amused. Some of the fountains met with opposition and the locals also created their own designs, which were even built (like the 'penis fountain' in Workum). Ultimately all 11 fountains were built. One of the nicest ones is the large open-mouthed fish by the American artist Mark Dion in Stavoren. Children love to climb into its mouth.

69 T-REX TRIX IN NATURALIS

Darwinweg 2
Leiden
South Holland
+31 (0)71 751 96 00
naturalis.nl

It all started with a young boy who sent his pocket money, five euro, to the director of Naturalis asking him whether he could use the money to buy the T-Rex that had just been unearthed in the United States. Following a crowdfunding campaign, titled 'a tenner for the T-Rex', the skeleton of the king of the dinosaurs finally came home to Leiden. She's actually a queen though and her name is Trix. She's 66 million years old and weighs in at 1700 kilos. A room was made especially for her at Naturalis, so you can marvel without distractions.

70 THE APENNINE GIANT OF MONDO VERDE

Groene Wereld 10
Landgraaf
Limburg
+31 (0)45 535 01 61
wereldtuinen
mondoverde.nl

You can travel around the world in one day in the gardens of Mondo Verde, catching your breath at a Russian *dacha*, a Japanese teahouse or an Italian villa. In the Forest of Follies, you will run into the 14-metre-tall *Apennine giant*, who is modelled after the 16th-century giant of the Italian sculptor Giambologna, which you can also see near Florence, in the Medici Park at Pratolino. It took four men seven months to carve this iconic sculpture from 470 tons of sprayed concrete.

71 SEA MONSTERS OF LEIDSEBRUG

Leidseplein
[Centre]
Amsterdam
North Holland

The *Sea monsters* of Leidseplein have been on a trip. To a stone cutter's workshop in Maarsen to be exact, where they were lovingly cleaned and fitted with new stainless steel anchors. Johan Polet's granite creations now proudly overlook the bridgeheads of Bridge 174, monitoring the busy gateway to the city centre. Once you notice these sea monsters, you'll discover plenty of other equally stunning creatures on Amsterdam's bridges, including Hildo Krop's creations. The public works department was of the opinion however that someone else should be given the opportunity to shine on this important bridge, which dates from 1925.

Great **THINKERS**

72 **EISE EISINGA'S PLANETARIUM**

Eise Eisingastraat 3
Franeker
Friesland
+31 (0)517 39 30 70
planetarium-friesland.nl

A minister from Franeker predicted that the world would perish in 1774. The wunderkind Eise Eisinga, who had already written a 650-page mathematical treatise at the tender age of 15, knew he was wrong however. That is why he spent years building a planetarium to show people how the universe really works. It opened in 1781. Eisinga, who originally was a wool dyer, based himself on the technique used to operate mills and relied on a Frisian pendulum clock to power it. You can also see the technology behind the planetarium in the attic.

73 **EINSTEIN'S WASH BASIN**

UNIVERSITY OF LEIDEN
Niels Bohrweg 2
Leiden
South Holland
+31 (0)71 527 27 27
universiteitleiden.nl

In the early 20th century, the University of Leiden was regarded as one of the world's most eminent natural historical laboratories. Hendrik Lorentz lectured there, as did all of the great physicians of the thirties including Niels Bohr, Robert Oppenheimer and Albert Einstein. All these geniuses washed the chalk off their hands over the wash basin in the lab. A student discovered this unassuming wash basin, after looking through archival documents. In 1997, the wash basin was transferred to the De Sitter Hall in the new Oort building, where it still hangs today and where you can go see it. Always check that there is no lecture in the hall before visiting.

74 **THE ESCAPE OF HUGO DE GROOT**

SLOT LOEVESTEIN
CASTLE

Loevestein 1
Poederoijen
Gelderland
+31 (0)183 44 71 71
slotloevestein.nl

Freethinker Hugo de Groot (Hugo Grotius) was one of the founders of international law. The fall of a political friend during the turbulent years of the Dutch Rebellion led to his lifelong imprisonment in Slot Loevestein in Gelderland, from 1619 on. His escape is almost as famous as his work. De Groot read stacks of books and was smuggled to freedom in the chest used to transport his books. The castle welcomes visitors. The chest in which he escaped now belongs to the collection of the Rijksmuseum in Amsterdam.

75 **THE HUYGENS FAMILY (AND THEIR DOG)**

HUYGENS' HOFWIJCK

Westeinde 2-A
Voorburg
South Holland
+31 (0)70 387 23 11
hofwijck.nl

Einstein supposedly once said that his theory of relativity continued where Christiaan Huygens had left off 300 years earlier. This savant discovered the ring around Saturn, and devised the pendulum clock, as well as the first *laterna magica* and the principle behind the Nike Air Max. The legacy of the intimidatingly intelligent father Constantijn and his son Christiaan Huygens is at the centre of their country house next to the station of Voorburg. If you search carefully, you'll find the grave where Constantijn buried his dog Geckie in the garden in 1682.

76 SPINOZA'S HOUSE

Spinozalaan 29
Rijnsburg
South Holland
+31 (0)71 402 92 09
spinozahuis.nl

Early renaissance philosopher Baruch Spinoza was born in the neighbourhood around Waterlooplein in Amsterdam. He did however spend part of his life in The Hague and Rijnsburg. He completed his famous *Ethica* in his home at Haagse Paviljoensgracht 72, where you can now visit the small library on Mondays from 2 to 4 pm. The Spinoza House is located in Rijnsburg, where he earned a living cutting lenses for optical instruments. In the late 19th century, it reopened as a small museum with his reconstructed book collection.

77 BELLE VAN ZUYLEN

ZUYLEN CASTLE
Tournooiveld 1
Oud-Zuilen
Utrecht
+31 (0)30 244 02 55
slotzuylen.nl

"I have no talent for subservience", said the freethinking noblewoman Belle van Zuylen to the Scottish writer James Boswell when he asked for her hand in marriage. During her lifetime, the work of this 18th-century writer and composer was already praised although she only shot to fame several decades after her death. The Literature Museum, in the Royal Library in The Hague, included her in a Pantheon of 100 highlights of Dutch literature. She was born in the medieval Zuylen Castle near Utrecht.

Fascinating **FANTASISTS**

78 **GEERT JAN JANSEN**
MUSEUMS VLEDDER
Brink 1
Vledder
Drenthe
+31 (0)521 38 33 52
museums-vledder.nl

The *Mona Lisa*? The *Night Watch*? Here in Drenthe? This museum in the former town hall of Vledder is home to the collection of Henk and Erna Plenter, who purchased a Matisse, which proved to be a forgery. Over time more collectors donated their bad purchases to the museum. Including some Karel Appels, some of which were probably painted by Geert Jan Jansen, the master forger who was arrested in the nineties with a French chateau full of forged artworks and who wrote a book about his career. On his website he refers to himself in the following not entirely unassuming way: "He has succeeded in making the entire international art world a laughing stock all on his own". Jansen visited the museum in Vledder and commented on the forged Appels but refused to be drawn out on which ones he had painted.

79 **BOUDEWIJN BÜCH**
NATIONAL MUSEUM
OF ETHNOLOGY
Steenstraat 1
Leiden
South Holland
+31 (0)88 004 28 00
volkenkunde.nl

Boudewijn Büch was a poet and novelist, and a Mick Jagger fan, who was devoted to Goethe. He became famous for his TV programme *The world of Boudewijn Büch,* in which he shared his knowledge about remote islands, the dodo, James Cook and of course Goethe in the most deliciously laidback style, all the while chatting away casually with his cameraman. His predilection for travel started in his childhood when he first visited the National Museum of Ethnology in Leiden, which is one of the world's oldest ethnographic museums. Here he felt 'more at home than at school', fantasising about distant places. Büch's encyclopaedic knowledge was paired with a lively fantasy: he invented an imaginary son (who died in childhood and whom he described in his novel *De kleine blonde dood*), a father who committed suicide and a million-dollar inheritance even though he was almost penniless in reality. Büch amassed a sizeable book collection in his town house along Keizersgracht, which was auctioned off after he died.

80 MATA HARI

FRIES MUSEUM
Wilhelmina-
plein 92
Leeuwarden
Friesland
+31 (0)58 255 55 00
friesmuseum.nl

Mata Hari was a self-made woman in an era when women were expected to resign themselves to their station in life. At the age of 18, Margaretha Zelle responded to a personal ad, marrying an officer of the Royal Netherlands East Indies Army, with whom she left for the Dutch Indies. After her divorce, she moved to Paris where she reinvented herself as an exotic dancer. She called herself Mata Hari, which is Malaysian, for 'eye of the day'. She was quite successful but also raised suspicion as a liberated woman, who travelled often and had many different lovers. She was executed by French soldiers for espionage during World War I. You can find her scrapbooks, the brooch with which she hoped to get in touch with her daughter again and letters in the Fries Museum in her native Leeuwarden.

81 LODEWIJK PINCOFFS

Handelsplein
[South]
Rotterdam
South Holland

Politician and businessman Lodewijk Pincoffs
(1827-1911) helped pave the way for the port in
Feijenoord. But this famous Rotterdammer also had
a tendency to fiddle his accounts. When his fraud
was revealed in 1879, he fled to New York leaving
debts to the tune of 9 million guilders behind.
He was rehabilitated in the nineties. The then
mayor of Rotterdam Bram Peper had a soft spot for
'naughty entrepreneurs'. Pincoff's statue stands
in front of his old office, which is now a boutique
hotel. He holds his hat in his hand very modestly.
The inscription at his feet reads: 'A spectacle of so
much glory and so much shame'.

82 ELVIS'S MANAGER

Veemarktstraat 66
Breda
North Brabant
Fietstour seeBreda:
+31 (0)76 700 25 99
seebreda.nl

Was he a brilliant manager or a shady businessman?
Dries van Kuijk, aka Colonel Parker, discovered
Elvis Presley and transformed him into the King.
It was a rather lucrative deal too because half of all
the earnings went to Van Kuijk allowing him to pay
off his gambling debts. The public prosecutor who
investigated Elvis's accounts after his death called
his actions 'unethical'. While van Kuijk claimed
for several years that he was an American, he was
actually born in Breda. Colonel Parker's former
home is one of the highlights of the seeBreda
bicycle tour. Nowadays only the annex, which is
now a shop, is still there.

**HAN VAN
MEEGEREN**

MUSEUM BOIJMANS
VAN BEUNINGEN
Museumpark 18
[Centre]
Rotterdam
South Holland
+31 (0)10 441 94 00
boijmans.nl

Johannes Vermeer's painting of *The Supper at Emmaus* was the discovery of the 20th century, a painting of unrivalled quality, according to all the critics. In 1937, the Museum Boijmans Van Beuningen decided to purchase it for 1,65 million guilders. But the painting proved a forgery, by an artist called Han van Meegeren. This master forger earned a fortune with his forgeries, even selling paintings to the Nazi commander Hermann Göring. The Museum Boijmans Van Beuningen is closed for renovation, but *The Supper at Emmaus* can be explored online at *boijmans.nl,* through video and photography.

Treasures from the
GOLDEN AGE

84 **THE DE PINTO HOUSE**

St. Antonies-
breestraat 69
[Centre]
Amsterdam
North Holland
+31 (0)20 370 02 10
huisdepinto.nl

In the seventies, the magnificent De Pinto House was almost demolished to make way for a dual carriageway (thankfully one council member voted against the plan). Instead the dwelling, which dates from 1605, was restored, and the classic interiors and opulent ceiling paintings preserved. The Jewish-Portuguese De Pinto merchant family lived here until the 18th century. Nowadays the building belongs to a cultural and literary centre with a library, which also hosts performances and exhibitions.

84 **THE DE PINTO HOUSE**

85 THE PEPPER HOUSE

ZUIDERZEE MUSEUM
Wierdijk 12–22
Enkhuizen
North Holland
+31 (0)228 35 11 11
zuiderzeemuseum.nl

The East India Company purchased the Pepper House in 1682 for the storage of pepper and other spices from Asia. Nowadays part of the Zuiderzee Museum is located here, which owns several historic boats and ships. A village on the Zuiderzee (the present-day IJsselmeer) has also been rebuilt here so you can learn more about Zuiderzee culture. The museum is also very popular with children.

86 VOC SHIP BATAVIA

Oostvaarders-
dijk 01-13
Lelystad
Flevoland
+31 (0)320 22 59 00
batavialand.nl

Shipbuilder Willem Vos spent several years pitching his idea to build a copy of a ship of the East India Company. Finally the municipality of Lelystad decided to go ahead with the project. He spent ten years building the *Batavia,* from 1985 onwards. This East Indiaman perished in 1629 off the Australian coast, with 40 members of the 300-strong crew drowning. Some of the survivors were also killed by the mutineers on board. The shipyard and the *Batavia* have since become part of the Batavialand Museum.

87 THE BLACK ARCHIVES

Zeeburgerdijk 19-B
[East]
Amsterdam
North Holland
theblackarchives.nl

In 2015, The Black Archives were created based on the legacy of the sociologist and writer Waldo Heilbron, who was of Surinamese origin but lived in Amsterdam. It is a growing collection of books and other publications by black authors and researchers about colonialism, racism and emancipation. The initiative for the collection was taken by a group of students and young people 'with a keen interest in a multicultural society', after years in which 'Black Pete' and the colonial past of the Netherlands were examined more critically.

86 VOC SHIP BATAVIA

88 SJAKIE'S CHOCOLADE-MUSEUM

Vlasmarkt 51
Middelburg
Zeeland
+31 (0)118 85 51 56
chocolatelover.nl

During the Golden Age, Middelburg in Zeeland was the centre of the cocoa trade until the merchant activities were transferred to Amsterdam in the mid-18th century (Amsterdam is still the world's largest cocoa importer). Here in this chocolate museum, you can smell, sample and learn all about the history of this sweet treat. The shop sells hundreds of different types of chocolate, some of which are produced in-house.

89 TROPENMUSEUM

Linnaeusstraat 2
[East]
Amsterdam
North Holland
+31 (0)88 004 28 40
tropenmuseum.nl

When the predecessor of the Tropenmuseum was founded in 1864, the founders hoped to compile a national collection of objects from the colonies. Nowadays the Tropenmuseum plays a pioneering role in the decolonisation of the museum world. It also pays a lot of attention to slavery and racism, with exhibitions about global cultural diversity, which are very accessible and which are also interesting for children.

Places to reflect on
WORLD WAR II

90 CORRIE TEN BOOM HOUSE

Barteljorisstraat 19
Haarlem
North Holland
+31 (0)23 531 08 23
corrietenboom.com

Casper, Corrie and Betsie ten Boom provided shelter to Jews, members of the resistance and other refugees. The resistance group to which they belonged to is estimated to have saved 800 lives. They were betrayed and arrested in February 1944. Only Corrie survived the war. Their house, which is the alternative Anne Frank House in a sense, is open to visitors from Tuesday to Saturday. The house can only be visited with a guided tour. Book online before visiting.

91 MUSSERT'S WALL

Hessenweg 85
Lunteren
Gelderland

The party building which the NSB had built in 1938 near the village of Lunteren in Gelderland was supposed to be 'a monument for eternity'. Only the wall, that was part of the stage on which party leader Anton Mussert gave his speeches, was retained. Currently there is a campsite here and now the prevailing idea is that *Mussert's Wall* is a national monument 'that reminds us of a dark chapter in our history'. Mussert only gave two speeches here by the way. Fuel was rationed when the war broke out and Lunteren was too far away.

92 THE HIDDEN VILLAGE

Pas-Opweg
Vierhouten
Gelderland
verscholendorp.eu

During the war a group of people hid in nine huts in the forest near Vierhouten in the Veluwe. The Hidden Village, which is also called Pas Op Camp (Attention camp), was discovered by chance by two SS officers who were out hunting on Sunday 29 October 1944. Some of the people were able to escape. Eight Jews were shot on the spot however. Three huts, some of which are half underground, were rebuilt along Pas-Opweg, approximately three kilometres outside of Vierhouten. Experience first-hand how dark and oppressive this shelter actually was.

93 WESTERBORK CAMP

Oosthalen 8
Hooghalen
Drenthe
+31 (0)593 59 26 00
kampwesterbork.nl

In the forties, approximately 100.000 Dutch Jews and other victims of the Nazi regime were transferred to this transit camp in Drenthe, from where they were transported to the extermination camps. The remembrance centre focusses on several personal stories from the camp. A bus drives through the forests to the former campsite. Although most of the buildings have been razed to the ground, the last remnants in combination with the impressive monuments combine to create an oppressive atmosphere. The observatory, with its 14 enormous telescopes, on the fringe of the campsite, that are used for astronomic research, only make the experience even stranger.

94 CASEMATE MUSEUM

Afsluitdijk 5
Kornwerderzand
Friesland
+31 (0)517 57 94 53
*kazematten
museum.nl*

Plenty of myths abound about the Battle for the Afsluitdijk, during which hundreds and possibly even thousands of German soldiers died. They are all wildly exaggerated. It was however the only battle which the Netherlands won after the Nazi invasion on 10 May 1940 (thanks to the bunkers of the fortifications of Kornwederzand and the support of the navy). After the destructive bombing of Rotterdam on 14 May 1940, the Netherlands ended up capitulating. The bunkers have since been transformed into a museum.

93 WESTERBORK CAMP

KUNSTMUSEUM DEN HAAG

BUILDINGS

Startling
BUS SHELTERS

---

95 SKULL IN DORDRECHT

A shelter in the shape of a skull: anyone waiting for a bus in Maria Montessorilaan in Dordrecht can wait under a huge skull designed by artist Joep van Lieshout. He also designed the bus shelter on the opposite side of the road, in the shape of an egg. The artworks *Alpha* and *Omega* symbolise birth and death. The skull especially elicited some violent reactions: the local newspapers reported that children at the nearby school suffered from nightmares because of this public transport art.

96 AMERICAN DINER

An American diner in the Veluwe? The rock 'n' roll fifties come to life in this asphalt plain, which serves as a transfer station. Anyone waiting for a bus here can listen to a jukebox filled with short stories. The real commuter is never bored here. They add 20 new short stories every year. *Short Story* was created by the artist Jerome Symons.

97 RIETVELD IN BERGEIJK

**Bushalte Hof
Bergeijk
North Brabant**

In the early 20th century the town of Bergeijk was a magnet for designers, who were associated with the De Stijl art movement. Gerrit Rietveld left his mark here as did the furniture designer Mart Stam and the landscape designer Mien Ruys. Waiting for a bus was never as stylish as in this Rietveld bus shelter, opposite a black and white Rietveld clock. Don't forget to visit the former De Ploeg factory (Riethovensedijk 20), which Rietveld designed, and the adjoining garden by Mien Ruys. You can easily find the building with the app or map of the Rietveld walk, which can be obtained from the VVV tourist office.

97 RIETVELD IN BERGEIJK

98 VIDEO BUS STOP REM KOOLHAAS

Emmaplein
Groningen

If you're waiting for the bus anyway, why not watch a video while you're waiting? Thanks to smartphones, this has become quite normal nowadays, but in 1990, when architect Rem Koolhaas designed this bus shelter for the Groninger Museum, this was still unheard of. The video wall is no longer in use unfortunately because of the intensive maintenance it requires. The words on the side of the bus shelter refer to the videos. There are plenty of other Koolhaas projects in Groningen. He designed the Brink flats, one of his earliest designs from the eighties, and a public toilet at Reitemakersrijge 22 for the *A Star is Born* city-wide event in 1996. Erwin Olaf's photos portray the battle of the sexes.

99 RIETVELD IN EINDHOVEN

Stadhuisplein
Eindhoven
North Brabant

Rietveld again, albeit in Eindhoven. He designed this bus shelter shortly before his death, but never saw the finished product. He devised a town pillar as a 'publicity medium' in front of the town hall: the town of Eindhoven used it for important announcements. This was 1964, so long before the days when municipalities published digital newsletters. Nowadays it is used as a mini-gallery. Famous Eindhoven residents such as comedian Theo Maassen and designer Piet Hein Eek have already exhibited their work here.

Romantic **R U I N S**

100 **BATENBURG CASTLE RUINS**

Molendijk 11
Batenburg
Gelderland
glk.nl/gebied/
batenburg

There is no place more romantic in the Netherlands than the Batenburg ruins, with its crumbling tower and overgrown walls, in the picturesque Land van Maas en Waal. In 1794, French troops set fire to the castle. It is probably one of the oldest castles in Gelderland although nobody knows when exactly it was built. The ruin already looks beautiful as you cross the moat. The ruin is occasionally open to visitors April through October, but it's definitely worth it to admire it from a distance.

101 **LICHTENBERG CASTLE RUINS**

Lichtenbergweg 2
Maastricht
Limburg

Only the tower of the medieval Lichtenberg Castle remains standing. The farm below it was built in the 19th century on the castle site. You can now access the tower through a new staircase, which has retained the run-down character of the site. The castle's high location on Sint-Pietersberg guarantees a stunning view, with Maastricht and the Maas on one side and the ENCI marl quarry and nature on the other.

102 VALKENBURG CASTLE RUINS

Daalhemerweg 27
Valkenburg
Limburg
+31 (0)43 820 00 40
kasteelvalkenburg.nl

The only castle in the Netherlands on higher ground was built from the 11th century onwards, in consecutive phases. The castle was irretrievably lost in 1672, a turbulent year, in which French, English and German troops invaded the Republic. The ruins are a nice place to visit. Look out for the awful round dungeon, which you were thrown in from above and from where you would never be able to escape. Be prepared, though, Valkenburg is very popular with tourists and can be busy.

103 ALMERE CASTLE (RUIN)

Oude Waterlandse-
weg 29
Almere
Flevoland

The ruins of a medieval castle in a polder that was only developed in the sixties. How is this possible? At the end of the last century, the local politicians felt Almere needed a nice wedding venue. Plans were hatched to demolish and move a French castle to the region but ultimately the planners opted for a new design, modelled after Château Jemeppe in Hargimont in Belgium. After some financial setbacks, construction stopped in 2002. Now and then, the plans are dusted off again. For the time being, the castle that was never completed, is still here, in verdant surroundings along the A6, to the east of Almere-Haven.

104 RUIN OF BREDERODE

Velserenderlaan 2
Santpoort-Zuid
North Holland
+31 (0)6 12 41 20 92
ruinevanbrederode.nl

The Zuid-Kennemerland National Park starts near the train station of Santpoort-Zuid. A 10-minute walk will take you to the remains of the 13th-century Brederode Castle. Its current state is the result of the Spanish siege of Haarlem in 1573, and some restoration during the 19th century. The ruin is open to visitors from March till November.

105 BROEREKERK

Broereplein 9
Bolsward
Friesland

This church in Bolsward, Friesland reopened after a tasteful restoration. It is all that remains of a 13th-century Franciscan monastery and burnt down partly in 1980. The church remained a ruin for approximately 30 years, until a glass canopy was built over it.

105 BROEREKERK

LIGHTHOUSES
for if you get lost

---

106 HET HOGE LICHT

Willem van
Houtenstraat 102
Hoek van Holland
South Holland
+31 (0)70 391 24 48
*kustverlichtings
museumhoekvan
holland.nl*

As a result of the increase in ships that called at Rotterdam, better coastal lighting was required near Hoek van Holland in the late 19th century. The 21-metre-tall red lighthouse, called Het Hoge Licht, was built at the start of the Nieuwe Waterweg. Nowadays this is a museum about coastal lights, with displays such as historic lighthouse lights and navigation equipment. Open from May till September on every first and third Sunday afternoon of the month. Or call for an appointment.

107 BORNRIF

Oranjeweg 57
Hollum
Ameland
Friesland
+31 (0)519 54 27 37
amelandermusea.eu

You must walk up 236 steps to get to the top of the 55-metre-tall Bornrif on Ameland, but the panoramic views of this Wadden Island more than make up for the effort. The island is still lit by the lighthouse at night. Nowadays the lighthouse keeper has been replaced with a webcam. The room on the top floor has been preserved in its original state. The lighthouse is open to visitors. Prepare for a short, steep climb. Check the website for opening hours.

108 DE LANGE JAAP

Zeeweg 5
Huisduinen
North Holland

Lange Jaap, measuring almost 64 metres, is the tallest lighthouse of the Netherlands and has been guiding mariners through the strait between Texel and North Holland since 1878. The bright-red lighthouse is situated between the Napoleonic fortifications of Fort Kijkduin and Den Helder. In stormy weather the cast iron tower moves slightly because of the wind.

109 NIEUWE SLUIS

Panoramaweg 1
Breskens
Zeeland
+31 (0)117 30 10 08
vuurtorenbreskens.nl

In the 19th century, Antwerp became one of the world's largest ports, which is why they petitioned the Dutch authorities in 1865 to make the Westerschelde easier to navigate for seagoing vessels. De Nieuwe Sluis guides ships through the dark night. The black and white lighthouse can be visited on weekends, from April till October and on Fridays, during the high season.

109 NIEUWE SLUIS

110 'T HOGE LICHT

Zuidstraat 1
Westkapelle
Zeeland
+31 (0)118 57 07 00
polderhuis
westkapelle.nl

In the evening hours, the light of the 't Hoge Licht lighthouse shrouds all of Westkapelle in a mysterious light. The tower is a mix of old and new. The base was originally built as a church tower in 1470. A fire in the 19th century destroyed the rest of the church, which was transformed into a lighthouse several decades later, in 1907. The light originally required whale oil to burn. Painter Piet Mondrian painted the lighthouse during his stay in the nearby artist village of Domburg. The lighthouse is open from April till November, on Wednesdays and Saturdays, and on Tuesdays and Thursdays in the evening.

110 'T HOGE LICHT

CASTLES *and* FORTS
with an exciting history

111 FORT RIJNAUWEN

Vossegatsedijk
Bunnik
Utrecht
+31 (0)6 54 91 64 24
fortrijnauwen.nl

You can find the largest fort of the New Dutch Water Line, an 85-km long defence, which was built between 1815 and 1870, just outside Utrecht. In case of an invasion, part of the Netherlands could be flooded and these 46 forts could protect the higher land. It never came to this of course. Following the development of new forms of artillery and airplanes, the line was already outdated a few decades after it was completed. The nature area around Fort Rijnauwen is a nice place for a walk or a canoe trip. A visit to the fort is only possible with a guide, on Wednesday morning, Saturday and Sunday afternoons, from April until October. The nearby Fort at Vechten (Achterdijk 12, Bunnik) was renovated when the Waterlinie Museum opened there.

112 DOORWERTH CASTLE

Fonteinallee 2-B
Doorwerth
Gelderland
+31 (0)26 339 74 06
doorwerth.glk.nl

It took 37 years to renovate and restore the 13th-century Doorwerth Castle to its former glory. This magnificent castle is beautifully located in green surroundings along the Lower Rhine just outside Arnhem. There is something to see in every room, including part of a medieval suit of armour, which you can try on, a museum about hunting, and rooms with works by artists who moved into the nearby rural towns in the early 20th century.

113 HERNEN CASTLE

Dorpsstraat 40
Hernen
Gelderland
+31 (0)487 53 19 76
hernen.glk.nl

In addition to the refectory and other historic rooms in this largeish and well-kept medieval castle, it's the 'forgotten' nooks and crannies that really appeal to the imagination. You can really lose yourself in the corridors in the attic, just under the roof and along the windows, if you use your fantasy and imagine that you are briefly in the Middle Ages.

114 RADBOUD CASTLE

Oudevaartsgat 8
Medemblik
North Holland
+31 (0)227 54 19 60
kasteelradboud.nl

Radboud Castle is beautifully located along the dike, with a view of the IJsselmeer. Count Floris V decided to build a defensive fortress here around 1283. From here the army was supposed to control the rebellious people of Friesland. This small castle used to be bigger at one time, just look at the foundations of the old corner turrets. The castle was renovated but the dungeons are just as dark and cold as ever.

115 FORT SABINA

Fortweg 1
Heijningen
North Brabant
+31 (0)168 47 17 59
fortsabina.nl

Napoleon ordered that this fort be built to protect his empire from English attacks from the sea. There was never any fighting near this section of the Brabant South Water Line, except when German special units captured two Canadian soldiers here during World War II, one of whom died in hospital. The ambience in and around the fort is very laidback. You can visit the inner and outdoor areas of the fort or the cafe-restaurant with its large terrace.

116 FORT KIJKDUIN

Admiraal
Verhuellplein 1
Huisduinen
North Holland
+31 (0)223 61 23 66
fortkijkduin.nl

Napoleon also built a fort at the tip of North Holland, which was built by local craftsmen and hundreds of Spanish prisoners of war. The 15-metre-long glass tunnel, which leads to the underwater aquarium where you can learn more about life in the North Sea, is especially surprising.

117 MUIDERSLOT

Herengracht 1
Muiden
North Holland
+31 (0)294 25 62 62
muiderslot.nl

Although the marketing department of the City of Amsterdam has renamed it Amsterdam Castle Muiderslot, Muiden was one of the most prominent cities of North Holland in the early Middle Ages. Following the growth of the powerhouse of Amsterdam, Muiden became part of the defence of the then Zuiderzee, and the 13th-century water castle looks just like it did then, ready to fend off an enemy attack. From April till October, you can also visit with a boat that departs from the Amsterdam suburb of IJburg (*amsterdamtouristferry.com*).

BRUTALIST

gems

---

118 FORMER HEADQUARTERS OF SC JOHNSON

Groot
Mijdrechtstraat 81
Mijdrecht
Utrecht

From the N201 in Mijdrecht, between Amsterdam and Utrecht, you might be forgiven for thinking that you are looking at a boomerang that floats above the water. Rotterdam architect H.A. (Hugh) Maaskant designed this building in the sixties for the American cleaning product company SC Johnson, which wanted a stylish building for its Dutch headquarters. Maaskant was known as the 'designer of the grand gesture', and a champion of the Nieuwe Bouwen style. Meaning: no bricks, just cement, steel and glass. He contributed to the reconstruction of Rotterdam, with his designs for the monumental Groot Handelsgebouw and the Euromast.

119 THE PROVINCIE-HUIS OF NORTH BRABANT

Brabantlaan 1
Den Bosch
North Brabant
+31 (0)73 681 28 12
brabant.nl

The building of the Province of North Brabant was architect Hugh Maaskant's last big commission. The 100-metre-tall, cement colossus was inaugurated by the queen in 1971 and has become somewhat of an icon along the A2 motorway. Maaskant was not interested in excessive interior ornamentation. Instead he preferred art that integrated with the building. Part of the collection – Karel Appel was in charge of the design of the cafeteria – is on permanent display. Following a radical renovation a few years ago, the building is now permanently open to the public.

118 FORMER HEADQUARTERS OF SC JOHNSON

120 AUDITORIUM TU DELFT

Gebouw 20
Mekelweg 5
Delft
South Holland
+31 (0)15 278 80 22
tudelft.nl

It doesn't get any more brutalist than this building, which is the auditorium of the Technical University Delft. This concrete edifice from the sixties looks both imposing and dynamic. The indoor space feels open and huge, the large auditorium protrudes over the main entrance. It was designed by architects Jo van den Broek and Jaap Bakema, two of the most famous modernist architects of the Netherlands.

121 TOWN HALL OF TERNEUZEN

Stadhuisplein 1
Terneuzen
Zeeland
+31 (0)115 45 50 00
terneuzen.nl

Terneuzen flourished after the war. And so the town thought it was time to build an iconic building for a modern port. Architect Jaap Bakema designed the town hall, which opened in 1972 and is located along the dike, with a view of the Westerschelde. The locals soon called it the battleship (they have several other nicknames for it). The stepped pyramid shape resembles a ship to a certain extent. You can easily imagine the captain surveying his surroundings from the top of the ship.

122 MINISTRY OF FINANCE

Korte Voorhout 7
The Hague
South Holland
+31 (0)77 465 67 67
minfin.nl

Two architectural styles in one building. When it was inaugurated in 1975, the Ministry of Finance was an ultra-modern office building, made of heavy and almost intimidating concrete. When the renovation was completed in 2008, the brutalist character was retained but the building was opened up and became more transparent. A glass canopy and a courtyard garden, that is open to the public, were added.

Early-20th-century
ICONS

123 MUSEUM HET SCHIP

Oostzaanstraat 45
[West]
Amsterdam
North Holland
+31 (0)20 686 85 95
hetschip.nl

In the early 20th century, the public works department of the town employed promising architects who would go on to leave their mark on Amsterdam, such as Joan Melchior van der Meij (the Shipping House), Michel de Klerk (Het Schip, De Dageraad), Hildo Krop (who designed the fantastic sculptures on Amsterdam's buildings and bridges) and Piet Kramer (bridges in Amsterdam, De Bijenkorf in The Hague). Het Schip, after a design by Michel de Klerk, is an undisputed highlight of the Amsterdam School, an expressionist architecture movement, which emphasised art and artisanship. A typical characteristic of this movement are the curvy façades, the decorative use of bricks and the rich detailing, including in the interiors. Het Schip is a real workers' palace, comprising three buildings, with 81 affordable rental apartments, and its own school and post office. Anyone could live in beauty and art, even if they didn't have much to spend in terms of rent. At least this was the prevailing idea at the time. Today people still live here. Het Schip underwent a thorough renovation in recent years, by the Eigen Haard cooperative. There is also a museum in the building where you can learn more about the living conditions of workers in the early 20th century and about the Amsterdam School.

124 **HILVERSUM TOWN HALL**

125 **KUNSTMUSEUM DEN HAAG**

124 HILVERSUM TOWN HALL

Dudokpark 1
Hilversum
North Holland
+31 (0)35 629 23 72
*dudokarchitectuur
centrum.nl*

W.M. Dudok was the city architect and director of public works in Hilversum and has more than left his mark on this city, with 75 designs. He designed garden cities, schools, cemeteries, bridges and a pumping station. His most impressive design, without a doubt, is the yellow-brick Hilversum Town Hall (1931), which is famous for its sleek horizontal and vertical lines and imposing tower. The Dudok Architecture Centre offers guided tours of the building from Thursday until Sunday, at 1.30 pm. On sunny days, you even get to climb the tower.

125 KUNSTMUSEUM DEN HAAG

Stadhouders-
laan 41
The Hague
South Holland
+31 (0)70 338 11 11
kunstmuseum.nl

H.P. Berlage died one year before this building was completed and inaugurated. While the Gemeentemuseum in The Hague dates from 1935, it looks very modern nonetheless, with a gallery between two ponds at the entrance, large spacious galleries with plenty of light and bright colours in the monumental hall. Visitors had to get the feeling that they were entering a temple of culture, away from the busy streets, where they would look at the works in every gallery with the same amount of attention. There is no signposted route in the museum because Berlage felt that you should lose yourself among the art. His design still works almost one hundred years later. The museum also has plenty of Berlage's designs on display.

126 RADIO KOOTWIJK

Radioweg 1
Kootwijk
Gelderland
+31 (0)55 519 16 65
hierradiokootwijk.nl

Radio Kootwijk looms up out of nowhere, like a stark colossus. As you emerge from the forest, you suddenly find yourself in a large, open space, as if a space ship just landed here. In 1923, this building was designed to provide a long wave radio link with Bandung in the Dutch Indies (today's Indonesia). A large transmitter mast with copper cables, which reached to the ground, was erected. But after just five years, this long wave technology was already considered outdated. The Amsterdam School architect Julius Luthmann was inspired by the Egyptian Sphynx and a transmitter station in Nauen, Germany for his design. Staatsbosbeheer regularly organises tours, but you can also visit the building on your own, from the outside, and take a walk in the nearby forest, heath and sand dunes.

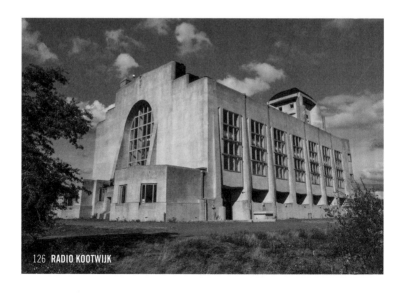

126 RADIO KOOTWIJK

127 VAN NELLE FABRIEK

Van Nelleweg 1
[West]
Rotterdam
South Holland
+31 (0)10 436 37 13
*chabotmuseum.nl/
rondleiding-van-
nellefabriek*

This imposing industrial complex, from 1931, is one of the icons of modernist architecture and was added to the UNESCO World Heritage List in 2014. It was designed by Brinkman and Van der Vugt architects as the 'ideal factory': transparent for the outside world, with plenty of daylight and pleasant working conditions. Guided tours of the building are organised on Saturdays and Sundays by the Chabot Museum. Buses leave from the museum at Museumpark 11. Do pay a visit to the Chabot Museum as well: dedicated to a local expressionist painter and located in a modernist villa.

127 VAN NELLE FABRIEK

Impressive
WATERWORKS

128 NEELTJE JANS / OOSTERSCHELDE-KERING

Neeltje Jans Island
Vrouwenpolder
Zeeland

In the night of 31 January 1953, a storm surge, combined with spring tide, flooded large sections of the Dutch coast. After the flood, in which just under 2000 people died, the Dutch decided to build large-scale coastal defences: the Delta Works, a large system of dams, locks and flood barriers, which took over 40 years to complete. Neeltje Jans is part of the Oosterscheldekering and was built in the river, as a 'production platform'. Here you can visit a large theme park and visitor centre, take a walk through the dunes and observe the bird population from the bird-watching hut, go to the (Proef Zeeland) fish shop, where you can buy Neeltje Jans mosselen. There's also a great snack bar.

129 AFSLUITDIJK

A7 between
Den Oever and
Kornwerderzand
North Holland /
Friesland
deafsluitdijk.nl

When you drive along the Afsluitdijk in the evening, you can spot the reflecting light gates by the artist Daan Roosegaarde at both ends. But you only get a real idea of the scale of this 32-kilometre-long dike in daytime. This was a gigantic undertaking at the time, sealing the Netherlands' reputation as a pioneer in the field of water works. In 1932, when the dike was completed, the Wadden Sea was definitely separated from the IJsselmeer, formerly the Zuiderzee. As such, this inland sea no longer existed from then on.

During the 1953 floods, the Afsluitdijk held back the water. To prevent future calamities, the Afsluitdijk will be raised and widened in the short term. There are plans to create a small passage for fish, so salmon can swim up the rivers again in the near future.

130 IR. D.F. WOUDA-GEMAAL

Gemaalweg 1-A
Lemmer
Friesland
+31 (0)514 56 18 14
woudagemaal.nl

The Netherlands' largest and oldest still operational pumping station can be found in Lemmer. It can pump up to four million litres of water a minute into the IJsselmeer if necessary. The pumping station is tested twice a year, which is a fantastic sight with all the steam. Learn more about the pumping station's history and functioning in the visitor centre. Want to see how it works? Check the website to see on which day the pumping station 'gets under steam', as they say.

131 WATERLOOPBOS

Voorsterweg 34
Marknesse
Flevoland
+31 (0)527 789 780
*natuur
monumenten.nl*

All these impressive waterworks are extensively tested before they are built. In the past, this was done in Waterloopbos in Flevopolder, where you can see various scale models that used to test the setting of the Maas Plain, the swell in a Libyan port, or the erosion on the Danish coast. The remnants of these test sites in the forest are now partially overgrown, and have become the habitat of birds and frogs. The old Deltagoot was transformed into a monumental piece of art, called *Deltawerk//*. Alongside you can find Paviljoen Het ProefLab//. This visitor centre is a good place to start your walk. Here you can also see one of the first wave machines that were used to mimic the effect of waves before they started using computers to do this.

132 MAESLANTKERING

Maeslantkering-
weg 139
Hoek van Holland
South Holland
+31 (0)88 797 06 30
keringhuis.nl

People flock from all over the country to see the long gates of the Maeslantkering close for a storm, even bringing a picnic. This storm surge barrier is one of the largest moving structures in the world: both gates are 210 metres long and 22 metres tall. But the Maeslantkering is just as magnificent when it is open. This storm surge barrier is part of the larger Delta Works, which protect South Holland, Zeeland and North Brabant against high tides.

133 GEMAAL LELY

Zuiderdijkweg 22
Wieringerwerf
North Holland

This electric pumping station, just outside Medemblik, is a hidden gem. It was completed in 1930 and is used to control the water level of Wieringermeer and protect the people who live in the polder. The engineer Cornelis Lely realised that the former Zuiderzee, an inland sea which is now called the IJsselmeer, could be cut off at Wieringen. The pumping station has been named after him posthumously. The Zuiderzee Works combine infrastructure with an aesthetic function. The resplendent white building in reinforced concrete, which was designed by Dirk Roosenburg (grandfather of architect Rem Koolhaas) is a magnificent example of the Nieuwe Bouwen style. The architects of this movement championed technology, functionality and austerity.

Heavenly **RELIGIOUS ARCHITECTURE**

134 BASILICA OF OUDENBOSCH

Markt 57
Oudenbosch
North Brabant
+31 (0)6 25 63 34 39
basiliek
oudenbosch.com

You can see this enormous basilica from a distance: it's as if you're gazing at St. Peter's in Rome, albeit in a town in North Brabant. The grandeur of the interior of this church, which was completed in 1880, is just as surprising from the inside. There are marble columns and statues of saints wherever you look, as well as an exuberant, painted cupola, and altar tomb beneath it, which was inspired by the original in the Vatican. An ambitious priest, who fell in love with the ornate architecture of Vatican City where he trained, came up with the idea for this building. He asked architect Pierre Cuypers, who designed Amsterdam's Rijksmuseum and Central Station, to build it.

135 SYNAGOGUE OF ENSCHEDE

Prinsestraat 14
Enschede
Overijssel
+31 (0)53 432 34 79
synagogeenschede.nl

In the twenties, the Amsterdam architect Karel de Bazel designed a new synagogue, at the request of a local textile manufacturer, combining art deco influences, the Amsterdam School and oriental elements with three characteristic cupolas. 700 of the 1200 Jews who lived in Enschede died during World War II. The fact that the synagogue, including the stunning mosaics and stained-glass windows, survived the war unscathed is considered a cruel irony by the council of the Synagogue: the German Sicherheitsdienst had moved into the building.

136 **WESTERMOSKEE**

Piri Reïsplein 101
[West]
Amsterdam
North Holland
westermoskee.nl

The Westermoskee opened in 2016, but it seems as if this house of prayer has always been here, in the early 20th-century Amsterdam neighbourhood of De Baarsjes. And it's not a small building either, covering a surface area of 1114 square metres, and having a 42-metre-tall minaret. The Franco-Jewish architects Marc and Nada Breitman were inspired by Ottoman architecture for their design. They also used typical Dutch bricks, which are also featured in the new apartments around the mosque.

136 **WESTERMOSKEE**

137 SINT BENEDICTUS-BERG ABBEY

Mamelis 39
Lemiers
Limburg
+31 (0)43 306 13 53
benedictusberg.nl

This abbey is devoid of any ornamentation. The stark design, the simple colours, the straight shapes and the muted blue-grey light that falls into the building through the windows, contribute to creating an extraordinary and soothing atmosphere, without distractions. The concrete exterior matches the grey interior. The only colour accent is provided by the green trees, which you can distinguish through the windows behind the altar. The atypical abbey of the monk/architect Dom Hans van der Laan, which was built in the fifties, exudes a sense of serenity and tranquillity.

138 SUFI TEMPEL

Zuidduinseweg 7
Katwijk aan Zee
South Holland
+31 (0)6 42 65 11 55
soefitempel.nl

The Indian Hazrat Inayat Khan, founder of the International Sufi Movement, saw the light in the dunes at Katwijk in the summer of 1922. He decided to rename this place, where he had such a spiritual experience, Murad Hassil, the 'place that fulfils sincere desires'. Universal Sufism brings an undogmatic message of unity and spiritual freedom. The Sufis continued to return to the dunes at Katwijk. In 1969, they built the world's only Sufi temple here.

Stupendous
BRIDGES

―――――――

139 MOERPUTTENBRUG

Deutersestraat
(opposite
Honderd-
morgensedijk)
Den Bosch
North Brabant

A 600-metre-long, 19th-century railway cuts through nature in De Moerputten, a stunning, wet low moor between Den Bosch and Geertruidenberg. It is no longer used which explains how it has since become a popular hiking trail with fantastic views of this marshy nature area.

140 SLAUERHOFFBRUG

Slauerhoffweg
Leeuwarden
Friesland

As if the road surface extends into the clouds: that's what it looks like when the Slauerhoffbrug is open. While movable bridge sections are not unusual in the Netherlands, this bascule bridge is raised by a huge counterweight. The roadway or slab of asphalt, which measures 15 metres by 15 metres, is positioned at an angle of 90 degrees, a few times a day because of the boats that pass through here.

141 MOZESBRUG

Schansbaan 8
Halsteren
North Brabant

As if Moses parts the seas before your eyes: this bridge runs through instead of over the water. The bridge was designed and built in just two months by RO&AD architecten. The idea was to make the bridge as invisible as possible. It is situated near the remnants of the overgrown 17th-century Fort De Roovere, which was part of the West Brabant Water Line. The surrounding area is worth visiting because of the varied landscape and the many country estates. It also has several signposted walks and cycling routes.

141 MOZESBRUG

142 THE WORLD'S FIRST 3D PRINTED BRIDGE

Between Boekelse-
weg (N605) and
the N272
Gemert
North Brabant

Brabant has plenty of unique bridges. Gemert has the world's very first 3D printed bridge, a collaboration between the Technical University of Eindhoven and the construction company BAM. The bridge is made from 800 printed layers of reinforced concrete and is strong enough to bear the weight of 40 lorries, even though it is for cyclists and pedestrians only. The TU/e also developed the technology for the first 3D printed concrete houses in the Eindhoven Meerhoven neighbourhood.

143 JOHN FROSTBRUG

Nieuwe Kade 23
Arnhem
Gelderland

In 1944, the allied forces made a brave attempt to liberate the Netherlands from the German occupying forces but Operation Market Garden was a failure and stranded near this bridge in Arnhem. The John Frost Bridge was literally a bridge too far. It was destroyed, rebuilt, destroyed again during the war and has since become an icon of the reconstruction and a lasting reminder of World War II and the many soldiers that died here.

144 ZALIGEBRUG

Between
Oosterhoutsedijk
and Ossenwaard-
pad
Nijmegen
Gelderland

A bridge that is designed in such a way that it is immersed a few days every year. Go see Zaligebrug by NEXT architects in the near of Nijmegen. Nowadays, rivers break their banks more easily due to climate change, which is why the alluvial areas have been extended in various places throughout the Netherlands, including at the Waal in Nijmegen. This meandering 200-metre bridge runs through a river park and connects the new Veur-Lent island with the Northern Waal bank. At high tide, you must use the stepping stones if you want to avoid wet feet.

145 **ZEELANDBRUG**

**N256 between
Zierikzee and
Colijnsplaat
Zeeland**

In the old days you could only get across the
Oosterschelde by ferry (which is still fun to do) but
as the ferry became busier, the longest bridge in
the Netherlands was built here between 1963 and
1965, between Zierikzee on Schouwen-Duiveland
and Colijnsplaat on Noord-Beveland. For quite
some time, this was Europe's longest bridge,
measuring 5 km, until Sweden claimed the title
seven years later with the Ölandsbron.

145 **ZEELANDBRUG**

CONTEMPORARY
BUILDINGS

146 PAVILION VIJVERSBURG PARK

Swarteweisein 2
Tytsjerk
Friesland
+31 (0)511 43 24 27
vijversburg.nl

Next to the 19th-century country estate, you'll find the largest self-supporting glass structure to ever be built in the Netherlands, namely the glass pavilion by Marieke Kums (studio MAKS) and Junya Ishigami. This beautiful visitor centre blends in subtly with the existing park. The glass façades are partly immersed in the soil and reflect the greenery, causing architecture to blend in with the landscape. The 19th-century park is also worth visiting, as it has gardens by Piet Oudolf and LOLA Landscape Architects and an art garden by the German artist Tobias Rehberger.

147 LOCHAL

Burgemeester
Brokxlaan 1000
Tilburg
North Brabant
+31 (0)6 42 65 11 55
lochal.nl

You can browse the bookshelves in this former gigantic locomotive hall, which has been transformed into a giant living room, enjoy a coffee, meet up with colleagues or attend a talk. The monumental building, which is situated behind Tilburg's Central Station, has been converted into a library and modern urban meeting space. The architect firm Mecanoo designed the interior. The Delft-based firm also designed Birmingham's new library and renovated New York Public Library's main branch along Fifth Avenue. The LocHal was an immediate hit with the locals when it opened and is always bustling with activity.

148 HOTEL INNTEL ZAANDAM

Provincialeweg 102
Zaandam
North Holland
+31 (0)75 631 17 11
inntelhotel
amsterdam
zaandam.nl

Some find it historicising kitsch, others think it's an amazing statement. Either way, you cannot ignore the Inntel Hotel in Zaandam, which is a fun collection of 70 Zaandam façades, which seem to have been stacked randomly on top of each other. All the houses are green, barring one: the blue house refers to Monet's painting *La Maison Bleue*, which he made in the Zaan Region. Wilfried van Winden's design from 2010 is a real eye-catcher and gave the centrum of Zaandam a boost, along with the urban planning design of Sjoerd Soeters.

149 NATIONAAL MILITAIR MUSEUM

Verlengde
Paltzerweg 1
Soest
Utrecht
+31 (0)85 003 60 00
nmm.nl

The building in the former air base of Soesterberg stands out because of its huge flat roof, which is supported by glass façades. There are no columns inside to obstruct your view. The immense hall (250 metres long, 110 metres wide and 13 metres high) is used to exhibit tanks, canons and military planes. The watchtower with a fabulous view of the Utrecht ridge crowns the building. This design by Felix Claus / Dick van Wageningen Architecten has already received several awards.

150 TOWN HALL OF DEVENTER

Grote Kerkhof 1
Deventer
Overijssel
deventer.nl

Aluminium replicas of the fingerprints of 2264 inhabitants of Deventer have been incorporated into the window frames of the town hall as a symbolic link between the population and the local government. The large open building by Neutelings Riedijk Architecten is designed around two courtyards and resembles a modern palazzo, that adjoins the old town hall. The result is a nice open space, with high ceilings, several colonnades and plenty of light.

151 BIESBOSCH MUSEUM ISLAND

Hilweg 2
Werkendam
North Brabant
+31 (0)183 50 40 09
*biesbosch
museumeiland.nl*

Studio Marco Vermeulen has completely renovated the old Biesbosch museum. Thanks to the national 'Space for the River' programme, it is now an island, with the museum as its centrepiece, which seems to have completely blended in with nature thanks to its green roof. The building is heated with willow wood and cooled with river water, or waste water that is purified with a willow filter. The interactive museum about the history of the Biesbosch, which was created following the Saint Elisabeth floods in 1421, is a really nice museum where you can learn more about the vegetation and animals that live here.

PLACES 🛈

INDUSTRIAL HERITAGE

with a second life

152 HEMBRUGTERREIN

Hemkade 18
Zaandam
North Holland
+31 (0)20 214 89 52
hembrugterrein.com

This former defence site was used as an arms and ammunition plant. The products were tested in the 'Plofbos' or explosion forest. The monumental industrial buildings are home to artists, designers, furniture shops, a food hall, restaurants and the exciting centre for contemporary culture Het HEM, which is located in a former munitions factory. It can be easily reached by bike or by bus from Zaandam station. A nicer option is to take the Zaan ferry from Amsterdam Centraal. Check the timetables before going (*zaanferry.com*) in that case.

153 STRIJP-S

153 STRIJP-S

Torenallee 1
Eindhoven
North Brabant
+31 (0)40 780 51 41
strijp-s.nl

Say Eindhoven and most people will answer Philips. This lighting manufacturer contributed to the development of Eindhoven. The former Strijp-S factory site is a perfect example of how to give an industrial site a new lease on life. You can see the newest art house films in the former physics lab (which Einstein visited!). There are plenty of original and fun shops in the Urban Shopper shopping centre (fashion, vintage furniture, bookshops, hairdressers) and you can quench your thirst and find a local, fresh snack to eat at the Het Veem market.

154 HONIGCOMPLEX

Waalbandijk 8-20
Nijmegen
Gelderland
honigcomplex.nl

You can still see the old logo of Honig, a sauce and soup manufacturer, which occupied the premises until 2012, on the side of the old flour silo. The plant is being renovated and a new residential neighbourhood is being built onsite. Currently the premises are occupied by a cultural centre, a restaurant, a coffee place and a beer brewery. Pop into the Oersoep Biertuin for a drink and a snack.

155 SPHINXKWARTIER

Maastricht
Limburg

A new city district is developing on the premises of the old pottery factory. A beautifully designed cinema, a concert venue, a branch of The Student Hotel, a furniture shop and 400 new dwellings must breathe new life into the 'Sphinx'. The Sphinxpassage with a 120-metre-long tiled wall tells the unique history of this site. Find out more about the Sphinx and the people who used to work in the plant in 26 chapters, made from 30.000 (!) tiles.

156 NDSM

[North]
Amsterdam
North Holland
ndsm.nl

Until 1984, they still produced ship parts and welded ships together on the wharves of the Nederlandse Dok en Scheepsbouw Maatschappij. New residential neighbourhoods were built in Amsterdam-North, especially for the NDSM workers. When the industry left, artists and squatters moved in, with trendy companies following in their wake. There are several nice restaurants with a view of the IJ (IJ-kantine, Pllek, Noorderlicht), a hotel in a crane (Crane Hotel Faralda) and interesting street art, such as the huge portrait of Anne Frank. Take the ferry from Central Station to NDSM.

Vibrant
NEIGHBOURHOODS

157 BELCRUM

Breda
North Brabant

In recent years, the main entrance of Breda's station has switched from the centre side to the north side, where the Belcrum neighbourhood is situated. A great way of integrating this once neglected part of the city more into the city proper. Now the magnificent Speelhuislaan leads you into Belcrum, which is populated with several former warehouses, with galleries like Electron, concert venues like Bloos, a popular skate hall, creative companies and fun spots for a drink, such as STEK and the Belcrum Beach summer bar.

158 INDISCHE BUURT / INDIAN NEIGHBOURHOOD

[East]
Amsterdam
North Holland

Legend has it that an official lobbied hard to get a hip coffee bar to set up shop in this neighbourhood, reasoning that the 'hipsters and yuppies will soon follow'. He was right. Javastraat and Javaplein have since become the beating heart of this neighbourhood, with its nice multicultural mix. Here you'll find a craft beer pub next to the Moroccan grocer, a hip barber shop next to an authentic pub and the Volendam fishmonger next to a Turkish baker.

159 OUDE NOORDEN

[North]
Rotterdam
South Holland

Old and new Rotterdam meet in Oude Noorden. You'll find all kinds of speciality stores in Zwaanshals, including a whisky shop and a wool shop, a vintage clothes shop, a beer brewer and nice restaurants. If you head over to Zwart Janstraat, you'll run into plenty of affordable shops for daily necessities, as well as shops that cater to the diverse population of this district, busy fast-food restaurants and old school pubs. And even a neon-lit karaoke bar, which more than lives up to its name, Salon Tropica.

160 ROTSOORD

Utrecht

In the past, the centre of Utrecht stopped at Ledig Erf. The former industrial neighbourhood was considered somewhat of a no man's land. Nowadays Rotsoord has had a new lease on life. You'll find a Berlin cafe and a speciality beer pub along Vaartsche Rijn as well as the De Helling concert venue. The Pastoe furniture factory has been here for quite some time. Nowadays it is occupied by art academy students, creative companies, and two restaurants, with a nice waterbound terrace.

161 SPIJKERKWARTIER

Arnhem
Gelderland

"From hookers to hip and happening", that is what the broadcaster Omroep Gelderland had to say about the transformation of the Spijkerkwartier. This used to be a red-light district (the largest after Amsterdamse Wallen) with plenty of crime and public nuisance. But nowadays the place is teeming with fun cafes and excellent restaurants. Café Vrijdag is very popular.

162 ZUIDWAL

The Hague
South Holland

There are two really nice streets between Den Haag Hollands Spoor station and Grote Markt, namely Bierkade and Boekhorststraat. Nowadays the stunning canal-side dwellings along Bierkade, which used to be home to such famous names as Paulus Potter, Jan Steen and Jan van Goyen (you can see their paintings in the Mauritshuis), are occupied by nice restaurants and a speciality beer pub. Boekhorststraat, which the city has designated as 'an authentic working-class neighbourhood', has plenty of vintage shops, a vinyl store and a bag shop. Do visit the Van Kleef *jenever* and liqueur distillery, which is situated just behind Boekhorststraat at Lange Beestenmarkt 109.

163 WYCK

Maastricht
Limburg
wyck.nl

It's easy to walk past Wyck, which is situated between Maastricht's Central Station and the first bridge over the Maas. If you walk up Rechtstraat, near Café Zondag, you'll automatically find it however. It's a quaint, old neighbourhood, with winding streets, plenty of clothes shops, vintage shops, speciality shops and places to eat or have a drink. A great place for a stroll in other words. This neighbourhood is all about the good life, something which the people of Maastricht are renowned for.

Extraordinary
CEMETERIES

164 AIRBORNE WAR CEMETERY

Van Limburg
Stirumweg
Oosterbeek
Gelderland

The bodies of more than 1750 young men who died during Operation Market Garden in September 1944 are buried here. This was an early attempt by the Allied Forces to liberate the Netherlands. They stranded at a bridge in Arnhem however. The majority of the graves are British, although there are also a few Dutch and Polish soldiers buried here. The bodies of the American soldiers who participated in Market Garden are buried at Margraten. The sight of the many simple tombstones emphasises the scale of the war and the many people who tragically lost their lives as a result all the more. The monument is inscribed with the words 'Their name liveth for evermore'.

165 HUIS TE VRAAG

Rijnsburgstraat 51
[South]
Amsterdam
North Holland
+31 (0)20 614 34 93
huistevraag.nl

Walk through the iron gate of the Huis te Vraag cemetery and you'll feel as if you've stepped into a different world. No graves have been added since 1962. The tombstones blend in with the surroundings and the silence is only interrupted by the chirping birds. You rarely run into someone on the winding paths, except perhaps a neighbourhood cat. There used to be an inn here in the Middle Ages. Legend has it that the Austrian Emperor Maximilian I stopped here in 1486 to ask for directions about how to get to Amsterdam. Hence the name.

164 **AIRBORNE WAR CEMETERY**

166 NOORDER-
BEGRAAFPLAATS

Laan 1940-1945 2
Hilversum
North Holland

The Noorderbegraafplaats was designed by
Hilversum's favourite architect W.M. Dudok and he
is also buried here. The buildings of this beautiful
green cemetery with its stately avenues are
typical of Dudok's style. When the cemetery was
completed in 1929, it was on the fringe of the city.
Nowadays the area is completely built up.

167 OUD EIK
EN DUINEN

Laan van Eik
en Duinen 40
The Hague
South Holland

Several prominent residents of The Hague are buried
in the city's oldest cemetery, including authors Louis
Couperus and J.J. Voskuil, painter Willem Mesdag,
politician Willem Drees and Nobel Prize laureate
and economist Jan Tinbergen. It's also a nice place
for a walk, with its old trees, magnificent tombs and
even a small ruin. These are the remnants of the
chapel that Count William II of Holland had built
for his father, Count Floris IV, in 1247.

168 HET OUDE
KERKHOF

Weg langs
Het Kerkhof 1-A
Roermond
Limburg
oudekerkhof
roermond.nl

Until recently, Catholics and Protestants in the
Netherlands did not mix and they were not even
supposed to marry each other. So the noble
couple that is buried in Oude Kerkhof cemetery
in Roermond must have had to cope with plenty
of indignation during their lifetime. They devised
a creative solution for the fact that they could not
be buried alongside each other: their monuments
shake hands over the wall that separates the
protestant section of the cemetery from the
catholic one. The famous Roermond architect
Pierre Cuypers (of Amsterdam's Central Station
and the Rijksmuseum) is also buried here.

169 **WESTERVELD**

Duin- en Kruid-
bergerweg 2-6
Driehuis
North Holland
+31 (0)255 51 48 43
bc-westerveld.nl

Tolerance is a quintessentially Dutch tradition. Something that is prohibited by law is allowed nonetheless. Cremation only became legal in the Netherlands in 1955. And yet the dead were cremated as early as 1914 here at Westerveld cemetery. This cemetery is home to the Netherlands' first crematorium, thanks to the 'Vereeniging tot invoering der Lijkverbranding in Nederland', an association which was founded in 1874. Here you can also find the urn of Eduard Douwes Dekker, the author of *Max Havelaar* who is better known by his pseudonym Multatuli, and the grave of Boudewijn Büch.

UNIQUE VILLAGES
that are worth the detour

---

170 BOOK CITY OF BREDEVOORT

Bredevoort
Gelderland
boekenstad.com

In the early nineties, this quaint village with its narrow streets was still very quiet. Too quiet even: many of the shops remained vacant. When a series of book merchants moved into the vacant buildings in 1993, this gave rise to a real 'national book city'. Bredevoort is now a bustling town once again, and has 20 unique (antiquarian) bookshops, including a German and an English bookshop, and a lively central square with a city brewery. An international book fair is held five times a year.

171 KOLONIEDORP FREDERIKSOORD

Frederiksoord
Drenthe
frederiksoord.nl

In the early 19th century, the 'Maatschappij van Weldadigheid' founded several so-called colonies for paupers. The poor who were unable to provide for themselves were sent to the east of the country, from the large cities in the west, by barge. There they were given housing, education, care and a job. Frederiksoord was the first colony and has remained pretty much the same after 200 years. You can see and read how the paupers lived in the Koloniehof Museum, download the 'Pauperpad' app or collect a map from the museum and hike through the lovely, forested surroundings. You can even spend the night in one of the colony's houses.

172 STEYL MONASTIC VILLAGE

Steyl
Limburg
kloosterdorpsteyl.nl

From the end of the 19th century, missionaries were trained in the monastic village of Steyl, from where they were sent out to convert the world. When they returned, they often brought amazing collections with them, including clothing, jewellery, utensils, drawings, sculptures and plenty of stuffed animals. You can find all these objects from China, Japan, Indonesia, the Philippines, Papua New Guinea, Ghana, Togo, Congo and Paraguay in their original displays in the Mission Museum. The convents, which were founded in 1875, are still occupied. There is also a beautiful Lourdes cave in the garden of the Mission House. Do visit the De Jochumhof botanic garden, or take a walk or a bike trip along the Maas.

172 STEYL MONASTIC VILLAGE

173 MODERNIST NAGELE

Nagele
Flevoland
museumnagele.nl

Nagele was the platform for experimentation for the architects of the Nieuwe Bouwen style, an icon of modernist architecture. This 'new town on new land' in Noordoostpolder served as a laboratory for the reconstruction. Famous architects such as Gerrit Rietveld and Mien Ruys designed various parts of this village, which explains why so many students and architects visit Nagele every year. Start your visit in the museum in the former church (Ring 23) or in the museum residence (Karwijhof 20). You can spend the night in a genuine 70s interior in the house next door. Check *monumentenbed.nl*.

174 VEENHUIZEN PRISON VILLAGE

Veenhuizen
Drenthe
veenhuizenboeit.nl

Like Frederiksoord, Veenhuizen was managed by the 'Maatschappij van Weldadigheid'. Not everyone accepted to be re-educated and assisted however, which is why three institutions were built here, which were later called prisons. Veenhuizen only opened to the public in 1981. Before this, only prisoners, prison officers and their families lived here. Visit the interesting Prison Museum!

175 VIJLEN MOUNTAIN VILLAGE

Vijlen
Limburg
bergdorpje.nl

The 1000-year old village of Vijlen is situated 200 metres above the Normal Amsterdam Level, the reference height. It calls itself the only mountain village of the Netherlands and it's a great place to start your exploration of the lovely, hilly landscape of South Limburg. Several (signposted) hiking and cycling trails start from Vijlen or run through it and wind their way through forests and fields to the adjoining villages. Stop at one of the many restaurants and cafes afterwards.

Charming
WALLED CITIES

176 WILLEMSTAD

VISITOR CENTRE
MAURITSHUIS
Hofstraat 1
Willemstad
North Brabant
visitwillemstad.nl

This quiet walled city was built in the 16th century, during the Eighty Years' War with Spain. The hiking trail along the green fortifications offers nice views of Hollands Diep. Here you can also find the oldest protestant church of the Netherlands. Start your exploration at Mauritshuis; this former city hall now functions as visitor centre and museum.

177 SLOTEN

Friesland
sloten.nl

The smallest of the Frisian Eleven Cities (famous because of the Elfstedentocht that passes through if the canals are sufficiently frozen) is car-free, classic and beautifully maintained. And yet, you never feel as if you've ended up in an open-air museum. People go about their daily life in Sloten even today. There are a handful of nice restaurants with a waterfront terrace and some quaint shops. Just outside Sloten, along Lytse Jerden road, is a small beach with sanitary facilities, from where you can take a plunge in Slotermeer.

178 HULST

178 HULST

Zeeland
hulstvestingstad.nl

There is something Flemish about the walled city of Hulst, which is beautifully preserved. The foundations of this city date from the 15th century, after troops from Ghent destroyed it. They were developed into so-called old Dutch fortifications in the 16th century. The earthen walls were able to withstand the heavier artillery and were less expensive to build than the stone bastions that were erected in Italy around the same time.

179 DOESBURG

Gelderland
bezoek-doesburg.nl

Doesburg in Gelderland feels very much like France on nice summer evenings. The city flourished for several centuries because of its strategic location along the IJssel. As a result, the medieval inner city has been well preserved. There are plenty of independent shops and busy restaurants in the city centre. Doesburg is also famous for its grain mustard and mustard soup. There is even a museum dedicated to this speciality in the Doesburgse Mosterd-en Azijnfabriek.

180 BOURTANGE

Groningen
bourtange.nl

Bourtange is probably the best example of what a walled city would have looked like circa 1742. This is largely due to the fact that the fortifications were rebuilt in the sixties – from the earthen walls to the soldiers' barracks and the wood toilets. The original fortifications were built at the end of the 16th century to repeal German attacks. By 1851, they were deemed redundant and demolished.

Former
ISLANDS

181 SCHOKLAND

Flevoland
schokland.nl

Schokland battled the water for centuries but was defeated by the poldering of the Zuiderzee. Nowadays it is listed as UNESCO World Heritage. Here you can see remnants of graves, the church and a museum about the struggle against the water, as well as fossils and archaeological finds (including a bear skeleton) from the surrounding area. It is not difficult to imagine that this place was once surrounded by water, when you look down from the village walls and see the large expanse of the Noordoostpolder at your feet.

182 WIERINGEN

North Holland
*wonderlijk
wieringen.nl*

Wieringen is like a Wadden Island, albeit without the tourists and the crossing. The narrow and sometimes overgrown roads wind their way around the former island, which was appended to the mainland in 1924. The hilly landscape is the result of encroaching land ice during the penultimate Ice Age. At the viewing point near Stroe you will suddenly realise that you are no longer looking at the IJsselmeer. Here you can really smell the sea. At the end of summer, you can spot black terns as they fly over. In the south of Wieringen, you can find the last Dutch dike built from seaweed.

183 **MARKEN**

North Holland

Due to its historic port, quaint wooden houses and the clog factory, tourists easily find their way to Marken. But you can get away from the crowds, by following the path around the former island. The 15-kilometre-long trail will take you through hamlets, with their characteristic, coloured wooden houses and Het Paard van Marken, the island's lighthouse. To the north, Bukdijk stretches into the water, like a 2-kilometre-long dead-end road. You can get to Volendam from Marken by ferry.

184 **URK**

Flevoland
touristinfourk.nl

Urk was an island in the IJsselmeer, until the dike to Lemmer in Friesland was completed in 1939. While this fishing village is more geared to tourists and pleasure boats nowadays, the fishing industry still has a prominent presence. The boats are maintained in the bustling port, where you can see nets drying in the sun and of course, you can eat good fish here. You can take a plunge in the IJsselmeer from the small sandy beach.

VIEWPOINTS
for phenomenal views

---

185 PLOMPE TOREN

Koudekerkse-
weg 12
Burgh-Haamstede
Zeeland
plompetoren.nl

You can already see the squat, reddish brown tower loom up from a distance: standing lonely, behind the dike in the wet Oosterschelde nature park. The tower is the last remnant of the flooded village of Koudekerke, which was abandoned in the 16th century. Only the church tower remained, as a beacon for ships. Natuurmonumenten has since opened the building to the public and is in charge of its conservation. Learn more about the tower and the park as you make the climb. The view from the top of the tower is simply phenomenal. If you're lucky, you may spot a porpoise or you can look at the seals through a telescope as they rest on the sandbanks.

186 DRIELANDENPUNT / TRIPOINT

Vaals
Limburg

If you are very good at Twister, then you should be able to put one foot in Germany, one in Belgium and one hand in the Netherlands, near the boundary post. The tripoint on Vaalserberg, which is the highest in the Netherlands (322 metres above sea level) has two belvederes: one on the Belgian side and one on the Dutch, near the restaurant. The parking lot on the Belgian side also offers a nice view of the valley.

187 **WINTERSWIJK STONE QUARRY**

Winterswijk
Gelderland

Look back in time, 240 million years to be exact, from the viewing point along Steengroeveweg, to the east of Winterswijk in Achterhoek. Several special fossils were found in this quarry. This area is unique in the Netherlands, with its mined limestone hills. Since 1932, they have been digging for limestone here. Since then, part of the quarry has been returned to nature. It's also the breeding ground of horned owls.

185 **PLOMPE TOREN**

188 PYRAMID OF AUSTERLITZ

Zeisterweg 98
Woudenberg
Utrecht
+31 (0)30 221 97 15
monument
*depyramide
vanausterlitz.nl*

A pyramid with an obelisk on top of it, on the highest point of Utrecht's hill range, built by the French general Auguste de Marmont, rather than by an Egyptian pharaoh. He was quartered in the region of Zeist, along with 18.000 soldiers, to fend off any British attacks. In 1804, he ordered that this monument be built, as an homage to Napoleon and to give his soldiers something to do. The pyramid is a reference to Napoleon's campaign in Egypt. The name Austerlitz refers to the Battle of Austerlitz, in the present-day Czech Republic. You can find the monument along the road from Zeist to Woudenberg.

189 KIEKKAASTE

Nieuwe Statenzijl
Groningen

A walk along a 600-metre-long boardwalk takes you from the locks of Nieuwe Statenzijl to the Kiekkaaste, a birdwatching hut on wooden post, along the reed beds. It is the only birdwatching hut outside the dikes in the Netherlands. To your right, you can spot the border with Germany and the sludge of the expansive Dollard, the mouth of the Eems River, lies at your feet.

Icons of the
WADDEN ISLANDS

190 HOTEL VAN DER WERFF

Reeweg 2
Schiermonnikoog
Friesland
+31 (0)519 53 12 03
hotelvanderwerff.nl

Time seems to have stopped here in this hotel, where you are served cups of filter coffee and piping hot bowls of pea soup in a brown taproom with Persian rugs on the table. The hotel rooms are furnished sparsely, with furniture from old houses. The former owner Sake van der Werff excelled at marketing, long before you could get a college degree in it, turning his hotel into a popular venue. He brought tourists to his hotel with a special bus, drew the attention of biologists and nature lovers to the stunning surroundings and wrote personal letters to prominent personalities. In 1936, he even decided to donate Schiermonnikoog to Queen Juliana and Prince Bernhard. It is said that Bernhard visited the place incognito at the time.

191 MUSEUM SORGDRAGER

Herenweg 1
Hollum
Ameland
Friesland
+31 (0)519 54 27 37

The *kakebienen* or whale jawbones in front of this museum are a lasting reference to the adventures of Ameland's whalers. A risky undertaking: the mariners would sail to the North Pole to catch gigantic blue whales with harpoons there. 1777 was a disastrous year, when several ships were stuck in the ice near Groenland. Hidde Dirks Kat kept an exciting diary about how some of his crew members survived on the ice floes and were saved by Inuit at the time. Learn more about the whalers in Museum Sorgdrager.

192 DRENKELINGEN-HUISJE VLIELAND

Vliehors
Vlieland
Friesland

It is quite strange to suddenly spot a wooden hut on posts in this expansive sand plain. This house was used by castaways who washed up here. Nowadays it has been transformed into a small museum about beachcombers. Vliehors is a strange enough area as it is. The village of West-Vlieland has been swallowed up by the sea and the plain is now used by the Ministry of Defence as a shooting range. So don't be surprised if you happen to stumble upon some shelled armoured vehicles.

193 HEARTBREAK HOTEL

Badweg 71
Oosterend
Terschelling
Friesland
+31 (0)562 44 86 34
heartbreak-hotel.nl

'Elvis is alive' and he lives a quiet life on the island of Terschelling. The fifties and rock 'n' roll come to life again here at Heartbreak Hotel. This beach pavilion, cum American diner, is a fun place to stop for a burger or a hot dog or an ice-cream sundae, sitting on red leather benches, while you listen to Elvis or Chuck Berry. Heartbreak Hotel is situated near the Boschplaat, one of the most beautiful nature spots on Terschelling.

194 LOLADZE GEORGIAN CEMETERY

Hoge Berg
Oudeschild
Texel
North Holland
liberationroute.com/pois/80/georgian-war-cemetery-loladze

The Netherlands were liberated on 5 May 1945, marking the end of World War II. Except on Texel, where the war continued unabated for another two weeks. A battalion of Georgian soldiers, who were prisoners of war, led by Commander Schalwa Loladze, from the Eastern front, had risen up against the German occupying forces in early April of 1945. An estimated 500 Georgians, 120 people of Texel and 800 Germans died on the 'last battlefield of Europe'. A majority of the Georgians who died here are buried in Loladze cemetery on Hoge Berg near Oudeschild.

UNDERGROUND
surprises

195 MAASTRICHT UNDERGROUND

Maastricht
Limburg
+31 (0)43 325 21 21
*maastricht
underground.nl*

Maastricht is just as multifaceted underground, with very high or very constrictive tunnels, wall drawings and a safe that was built during World War II to store 750 art treasures, including *The Night Watch* and 42 other works by Rembrandt, Paulus Potter's *The Bull* and Vermeer's *The Little Street*. The caves of Sint-Pietersberg were for the most part dug in marl by human hands. The mountain also has an underground tunnel to the 18th-century fortifications. Maastricht Underground offers guided tours of these unique places. You can book through the website.

196 A BOAT TRIP ON THE BINNENDIEZE

TICKETS:
Parade 12
Den Bosch
North Brabant
+31 (0)73 613 50 98
dagjedenbosch.com

The city looks quite different from the water, especially when you are sailing under the buildings, as you can do in Den Bosch. The Binnendieze, a network of small canals, winds its way through the city. In the past, people often built over the water to compensate for the lack of space for urban expansion. The trip (available from April until October) will take you from open water under the sometimes constrictive overpasses to places where a house has been built on the water and even under the choir of St. Catherine's Church.

197 THE 'SECRET' NATO HQ

Cannerweg 798
Maastricht
Limburg
+31 (0)77 473 75 75
limburgs-landschap.
nl/natuurgebied/
cannerbos

The former marl quarry in Limburg's Cannerberg has a Mainstreet and a Bravostreet. In the fifties, they were part of the 'ultra-secret' NATO Headquarters. Initially this was a temporary base, but it became permanent after the Berlin Wall was built. From here NATO stayed in contact with the troops that had to defend the north of Germany against the Russians in case of war, and with the war planes that would provide support to them. In 1993, the organisation left the base. The doors swing open once a month to the public. You can book through the website.

198 MAAS TUNNEL

Charloisse Hoofd/
Parkkade
Nieuwe Werk/
Charlois
[West/South]
Rotterdam
South Holland
maastunnel.nl

It is always a strange sensation to walk or cycle 20 metres beneath the Nieuwe Maas River. Until well into the 19th century, the only way to get from the north of Rotterdam to the south of the city was by ferry. A bridge would disrupt shipping. When the bridges were finally built, it soon became clear that more capacity was needed. The first road tunnel in the Netherlands was inaugurated in 1942. At the end of the war, the Germans attempted to blow up the tunnel but the resistance was able to prevent this.

199 DOMUNDER

Domplein 4
Utrecht
+31 (0)30 236 00 80
domunder.nl

All of Utrecht's history converges underground, from the remnants of the Trajectum Roman fort to a medieval cellar and the destruction caused by a tornado in 1674. DOMunder, an interactive museum and historical attraction, which is located five metres under Utrecht's Domplein wants to offer visitors an immersive experience, giving them the sensation that they are archaeologists working underground. You will be given a torch to shine light on the finds in the soil.

200 RIJSWIJK COMMAND POST

Van Vredenburch-
weg 176-A
Rijswijk
South Holland
+31 (0)6 18 30 28 05
museumbescherming
bevolking.nl

The Park Overvoorde bunker complex is situated just outside The Hague and has two underground command posts. The bunker was built during World War II and used as an atomic bunker from 1969 onwards. There are very few bunkers that are still in such good shape as this one, which was restored to its former glory and is now home to a museum.

LIFE ACHIEVEMENTS
worth admiring

201 NATURA DOCET WONDERRYCK TWENTE

Oldenzaalse-
straat 39
Denekamp
Overijssel
+31 (0)541 35 13 25
wonderryck.nl

In 1911, a schoolmaster called Bernink set up an early form of a crowdfunding campaign to fund a museum of natural history in his parental home. He was fascinated by nature all his life, establishing collections and teaching himself the art of taxidermy to stuff animals for display. In 1922, Natura Docet (nature teaches) expanded into the current museum villa along Oldenzaalsestraat. Here you can still feel the mind of a passionate collector and nature lover at work. The museum's collection includes plants and animals from Twente and the rest of the world as well as an impressive collection of fossils.

202 THE DUTCH KREMLIN

Limmerschouw 51
Winkel
North Holland
+31 (0)224 54 15 98
*kunsttuinnederlands
kremlin.nl*

Yes, it's not your imagination, you are looking at the Kremlin, tucked in between a golf course and Provincialeweg. Since 1980, Ger Leegwater has been working on this art garden, near his house, in the North Holland village of Winkel. Walk past dragons and sarcophagi, Greek gods and biblical figures, chapels and the fairy-tale centre of Russia's government. The garden is not always open, so check the website for open garden days. Peek through the gates and you'll get a good idea of what's on display here.

203 MIRAMAR SEA MUSEUM

Vledderweg 25
Vledder
Drenthe
+31 (0)521 38 13 00
miramar-
zeemuseum.nl

It's never too late to change careers as Jeanne Warners proved. She was 55 years old, her mother had just died when she happened to pick up a unique shell on a beach in Mallorca and discovered her ambition in life: to found her own sea museum so everyone could enjoy this 'unknown beauty'. Miss Warners visited over 80 countries, until her death in 1986, armed with a large trunk on the undercarriage of a pram. She spent the summers working on her museum while searching for shells, fish and other ocean treasures during the winter months. Her journeys are depicted on the large map in the reconstructed study in her museum in Vledder, in Drenthe. Her stuffed monkey Kabouter keeps an eye on visitors, from his own display case. The museum consists of her own collection and donations.

204 ECOCATHEDRAL

IJntzelaan
Mildam
Friesland
+31 (0)6 24 57 30 20
ecokathedraal.nl

In 1966, the landscape architect (or 'ecotect') Louis Le Roy built his first ecocathedral, a landscape artwork, in which man and nature coexist in harmony. He further developed his ideas in the nearby village of Mildam, where he planted trees and built the mother of all ecocathedrals, from old tiles and construction waste. Le Roy died in 2012, but volunteers continue his life's work on Tuesday afternoons. Admission to the cathedral is free. The first Le Roy garden is situated along President Kennedylaan and Europalaan in Heerenveen.

205 CACTUSOASE THEME PARK

Jongermanssteeg 6
Ruurlo
Gelderland
+31 (0)573 45 18 17
cactusoase.nl

In the early seventies, Anny and Bert capitalised on the first wave of popularity of the cactus, doing brisk business as a result. But when cheap cactuses from Southern Europe flooded the market, they decided to transform their 6000 square metres of greenhouses into a cactus theme park. See 'Anny's children', a collection of cactuses in all sizes and shapes, which Anny grew over the years. They also created a space for the local model train association, the historical society and artists. Bert built his own cactus pyramid, which is home to a collection of minerals. We bet you'll be unable to resist Anny's infectious enthusiasm, and will leave with a cactus and plenty of care tips.

206 JOPIE HUISMAN MUSEUM

Noard 6
Workum
Friesland
+31 (0)515 54 31 31
jopiehuisman
museum.nl

The eccentric artist Joop Huisman became famous in the seventies with his realistic paintings of Frisian landscapes and ordinary people. A museum opened during his lifetime in his native Workum. 'Jopie', who was a self-taught artist, rarely sold works as he felt that their value could not be expressed in monetary terms. You can also see some of the objects he regularly featured in his paintings here, including a pair of secondhand shoes he received and continued to use for over 40 years.

Phenomenal
PORTS

207 HISTORIC DELFSHAVEN

[West]
Rotterdam
South Holland
historischdelfshaven
rotterdam.nl

Tourists sometimes refer to Historic Delfshaven as 'just like Amsterdam', but the small port is a typical old-Dutch port. This hidden part of Rotterdam is populated with old warehouses and a mill that reminds visitors of the once flourishing *jenever* industry. In the early 17th century, the Pilgrim Fathers left from here on the Speedwell to found New England in the New World. The Pilgrim Fathers Church attests to this. The nearby De Pelgrim brewery is also worth visiting.

208 PIUSHAVEN

Tilburg
North Brabant
piushaven.nl

Tilburg's Piushaven must have been teeming with people in the previous century. After the war, however, rail transport became more popular and the port was neglected. In recent years, the port buildings have been restored, new homes have been built and restaurants and pubs have moved in, taking advantage of the central waterfront location.

209 NOORDERHAVEN

Harlingen
Friesland

The historic Noorderhaven of Harlingen in Friesland has been a bustling port for several centuries. Nowadays, pleasure boats moor here, but in the old days ships from around the world would call here. Just look at the names of the warehouses: Poland, Russia, Sumatra. You can also catch the boat to Terschelling nearby.

209 NOORDERHAVEN

210 HAVENKWARTIER

Scheepvaartstraat
Deventer
Overijssel
havenkwartier
deventer.com

There were plans to redevelop this port area along the IJssel, with apartment buildings and villas. But the nearby industry prevented this. Instead, a space was created for 'people with ideas'. The result is a lively city district, which is home to artists and other creative minds, pubs and restaurants and small companies.

211 VLISSINGEN

Zeeland

The centuries-old port city of Vlissingen has the largest sea boulevard in the Netherlands, which offers stunning views of the Westerschelde. From there, it's just a short walk to the beach. There are plenty of pubs and restaurants near the inner port, along Nieuwendijk. But the best way to experience a port city is from the water, by water taxi.

212 OUDE HAVEN

Zierikzee
Zeeland

Walk through the medieval city gates to enter the old port of picturesque Zierikzee, where plenty of historic sailing and motorboats are moored. You can also see sections of the old city walls here, which, like the hundreds of monuments in Zierikzee, refer to this city's prosperous past as a merchant city.

EXCALIBUR OUTDOOR CLIMBING WALL

ACTIVITIES 👣

Awesome places for
WATER SPORTS

---

213 SAILING ON SLOTERMEER
Balk
Friesland

Slotermeer connects the Frisian lakes with the Gaasterland nature area. The calm and clear water make this an excellent place for a swim. You'll sometimes run into some boats or surfers here too. Balk has several boat rental companies, where you can rent a valk or an optimist. Sloten, one of the Frisian Eleven Cities, is a lovely village and definitely worth visiting.

214 KITESURFING IN IJMUIDEN
IJmuiden
North Holland

Kitesurfing or kiteboarding is much easier to learn than surfing or windsurfing and is great fun from the minute you start. The kite propels you across the water on your board allowing you to achieve amazing speeds. IJmuiden has a wide beach and the sea is always within arm's reach. The water is relatively shallow here and because IJmuiden is located at the mouth of the North Sea Canal it's a good place to kitesurf in any wind. There are different kitesurfing schools for beginners and people who want to rent equipment.

215 SURFING NEAR WIJK AAN ZEE
Noordpier
Wijk aan Zee
North Holland

Wijk aan Zee has the best waves in the Netherlands, which is why it is a hotspot for surfers. Surfschool Ozlines, near the Timboektoe beach pavilion, organises classes, including for children, or group sessions for families.

216 CANOEING IN THE WEERRIBBEN-WIEDEN

Overijssel
visitweerribben wieden.com

The Weerribben-Wieden National Park is a large peat bog in the province of Overijssel. Here you can sail across open lakes, past dense reed belts and along channels that are almost hidden from view because of the bankside growth. You can rent a canoe in Kalenberg, Ossenzijl and Giethoorn (the 'Venice of the Low Countries'). Spending the night in the park can also be a lot of fun. There are special canoe campsites, which are allocated by Natuurmonumenten, as well as ordinary campsites. You can download various canoe routes from the website.

217 SUP SURFING IN LEEUWARDEN

Leeuwarden
Friesland
+31 (0)582 03 83 99
supskool leeuwarden.nl

Stand-Up-Paddling means using a paddle to speed through the water on a longboard. It's a deliciously relaxing activity, which gives you a completely different perspective of the city. SUP is becoming increasingly popular in the Netherlands. You can rent a board, take a class or join a tour at SUP Skool Leeuwarden.

218 DIVING IN THE OOSTERSCHELDE

Oosterschelde
Zeeland
duikeninzeeland.nl

Squid, seahorses, North Sea crabs, large cod and seals: you can see all of the above and more if you go diving in the Oosterschelde, which is the Netherlands' most diverse diving location. If you decide to dive at Plompe Toren near Burgh-Haamstede, you will even see the remnants of the drowned village of Koudekerke underwater. The Duiken in Zeeland diving school will give you more information about the various diving locations and organises guided dives.

See Mother Nature
ON TWO WHEELS

---

219 KENNEMER DUNES

**Overveen/
Bloemendaal
North Holland**
*np-zuidkennemer
land.nl*

Where else can you spot a large fallow deer on the dunes, see European bison calmly grazing or catch a glimpse of a stonechat as it surveys its surroundings? The Kennemer Dunes, which are part of the Zuid-Kennemerland National Park, are within cycling distance of Haarlem and Amsterdam. This stunning nature area, which is near the North Sea, has plenty of magnificent old country estates. Go to *nederlandfietsland.nl* to download a map of the signposted 25-kilometre route, which passes several cycle junctions.

220 A TOUR OF THE DIEFDIJK LINE

**Everdingen tot
Kedichem
South Holland/
Gelderland**
*culemborg.fietsers
bond.nl/fiets
tochten-2/rondje-
diefdijk-39-of-65-km*

The Dutch Water Line cuts through South Holland and Gelderland and consists of a series of water-based defences, which can be used to flood the land in case of danger. Cycle along the Diefdijk Line to explore a typical Dutch landscape. En route, you will run into Bunker 599 along the Diefdijk near Culemborg: this bunker has been sawn in two and also has a jetty. At Meerdijk you can visit a reconstructed trench. A description of the route (39 or 65 km) can be found on the website.

221 BELS LIJNTJE

**Tilburg to
Turnhout
North Brabant/
Belgium**

The locals call the train from Tilburg to Turnhout
the 'Bels lijntje'. It connects Brabant with the
Kempen Region in Belgium. Nowadays it is also
a bike route. The long, straight tour winds its way
past old train stations and through Baarle-Nassau
and Baarle-Hertog, the village where the border
between Belgium and the Netherlands actually
runs through houses.

222 RONDJE PONTJE

**Arnhem-Nijmegen
Gelderland**
*nederlandfiets
land.nl/fietsroute/
rondje-pontje-
fietsroute*

A lovely 40-kilometre route that will take you
past the Waal, the Rhine, the Pannerdensch Canal
and the Linge. En route, you will have to take
a ferry three times. You will also bike past a fortress,
a castle and a tea garden in Millingerwaard and
run into large grazers. Check the timetables of
the ferries before leaving. The website includes
a description of the 'Rondje Pontje' tour and a link
to the time-tables.

223 WADDEN SEA
ROUTE LF10

**Callantsoog to Bad
Nieuweschans
North Holland –
Groningen**

This 270-kilometre Wadden Sea Route is part of
the much longer international North Sea Route.
You can also choose to follow parts of the route,
which is excellently signposted; look out for the
square white LF10 signs. It will take you past
several beauty spots along the Wadden Coast, over
dikes, past Frisian mounds and Groningen country
estates, and along the Afsluitdijk to the tip of
North Holland.

224 GULPEN ORGANIC CYCLING ROUTE

Heerlen – Vijlen
Limburg
fietsnetwerk.nl

While the landscape in the Netherlands is largely flat, South Limburg is the welcome exception to the rule. This cycling tour, which will take you past farms, vineyards and castles, winds its way up and down the hills and through the towns of Gulpen, Vijlen, Valkenburg and the city of Heerlen. Check the website for a map of the route, listing cycle junctions and places to stop. A recommended stop is the Gulpener Brouwlokaal, with a fantastic beer garden complete with hop plants.

225 BREDE DUINEN ROUTE

Alkmaar – Bergen – Schoorl
North Holland
routeindex.nl/route/
fietsroutes/fietsen/
brede-duinen-route-
anwb/9379

This bicycle route, which passes through forests, past high dunes, and through heaths, was previously voted 'the best cycling route of the Netherlands'. Bike through the expansive dunes of Schoorl, over the Hondsbossche Zeewering (a well-known sea dike) and through a bird reserve. The website includes a detailed description. This 45-kilometre route begins and ends in Alkmaar.

Day trips that put
A SMILE ON KIDS' FACES

---

226 BOOMKROONPAD
BUITENCENTRUM
BOOMKROONPAD
Steenhopenweg 4
Drouwen
Drenthe
+31 (0)592 37 73 05

Experience the forest from a different perspective. Buitencentrum Boomkroonpad is an outdoor adventure centre on the Hondsrug, the sandbank that extends from Emmen to Groningen. Here you can take a short treetop walk while a guide tells you more about the nature around you. The highest point is approximately 22 metres above the sea level. It's also a great area for a walk and they also have a nature treasure hunt and a gnome path for small children.

227 BIRD REHABILITATION CENTRE
Luitertweg 36-A
Zundert
North Brabant
+31 (0)76 597 41 65
vrczundert.nl

The Bird Rehabilitation Centre in Zundert takes care of injured birds or babies that were pushed out of their nests as well as other wildlife including roebucks and hedgehogs. Since 1980, they lovingly tend to all kinds of creatures in large enclosures in green surroundings, making this a great place for a walk. You can see plenty of special birds here such as an eagle owl or a curious raven. The centre also invests in education, with school visits and guided tours, and has a nice nature shop. Check the website for opening times.

226 **BOOMKROONPAD**

228 MUSEUM DE HEKSENWAAG

Leeuweringer-
straat 2
Oudewater
Utrecht
+31 (0)348 56 34 00
heksenwaag.nl

For several centuries, witches were weighed here in the Oudewater Witches Weighhouse. If you were too light, you were considered a witch. If the weighing test showed that you were not a witch, you received a certificate to prove your innocence. In 1545, Emperor Charles V granted Oudewater the privilege to organise these witch-weighing tests, as the only European weighhouse. This tiny museum in the historic village of Oudewater tells the history of the witches' trials in early modern Europe. Once you have visited the museum, you can ask to be weighed on the original scales. If you are innocent, you will get a certificate to take home with you.

229 ZEEHONDEN-CENTRUM PIETERBUREN / SEAL REFUGE

Hoofdstraat 94-A
Pieterburen
Groningen
+31 (0)595 52 65 26
zeehondencentrum.nl

This seal refuge, which was founded in 1971, used to be called the seal nursery because it mainly cared for 'wailers' that had been left behind by their mums on the mudflat, where they were usually found crying inconsolably. Now that the seal population has flourished, the centre has revised its policy of care for these creatures. Get up close and personal with the seals, before they are released into the wild again. You can even assist with their release. The refuge is set to move to the new Waddencentrum in Lauwersoog in the near future.

230 CORPUS

**Willem
Einthovenstraat 1
Oegstgeest
South Holland
+31 (0)71 751 02 00**
corpusexperience.nl

Whereas other museums are gradually switching to more interactive presentations, Corpus was an interactive experience from the outset. Take a journey through the human body in this unique building, which you can spot from a distance. Take the escalator up, into the gut. Elsewhere spermatozoids will speed past and you can follow red blood cells as they are propelled through the heart and arteries.

231 GEOFORT

**Nieuwe Steeg 74
Herwijnen
Gelderland
+31 (0)345 630 480**
geofort.nl

Learn more about maps, navigation, tracking and treasure hunts in the GeoFort. While this may sound like an old-fashioned museum in the era of Google Maps, it is a fun, interactive and instructive experience nonetheless. After your visit to this old fort, which is part of the New Dutch Water Line, you'll know how the GPS on your smartphone works or how a salmon finds its way to its spawning grounds. In 2016, GeoFort was voted the world's best children's museum.

ADRENALINE KICKS
for daredevils

232 EXCALIBUR OUTDOOR CLIMBING WALL

KLIMCENTRUM BJOEKS
Bieskemaar 3
Groningen
+31 (0)50 549 12 30
bjoeks.nl

Experienced climbers can test their skills on one of Europe's highest climbing walls at Climbing Center Bjoeks near the Kardingerplas. Their intimidating outdoor Excalibur tower is 37 metres tall and has an 11-metre overhang. Fanatics can pitch up their tent at the foot of the tower for free. You can even sleep on the top of the tower if you like a real adrenaline rush. At your own risk of course.

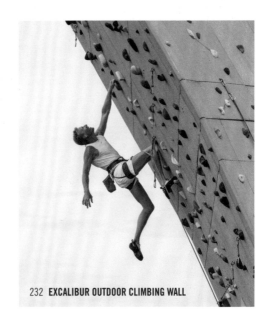

232 EXCALIBUR OUTDOOR CLIMBING WALL

233 ABSEILING OR ZIP-LINING FROM THE EUROMAST

233 ABSEILING OR ZIP-LINING FROM THE EUROMAST

Parkhaven 20
[West]
Rotterdam
South Holland
+31 (0)10 436 48 11
euromast.nl

The Euromast is the tallest publicly accessible tower in the Netherlands and an icon of Rotterdam's impressive skyline. The tower, which was built in 1960, is open to the public. It has a restaurant on the 100-metre level and a viewing platform at 185 metres. Real daredevils can take a more unorthodox way down (only in the summer months). Use the zip line to get to ground level in just 15 seconds at a speed of 100 km/hour. Abseiling takes a little longer.

234 BUNGEE JUMPING FROM THE PIER

Strandweg 150
Scheveningen
South Holland
+31 (0)70 221 11 38
bungy.nl

The North Sea's waves come closer at a daunting speed. And then, just in time, the elastic retracts and you are propelled back into the air. The Pier of Scheveningen is the only permanent location for a bungee jump in the Netherlands. You jump 60 metres down, with a view of the beach and the boulevard.

235 CAVE BIKING

Oud Valken-
burg 2-A
Schin op Geul
Limburg
+31 (0)43 604 06 75
aspadventure.nl

Let's hope your lamps won't die during your cave biking tour in Valkenburg because Limburg's marl caves are pitch-dark. The 10K tour lasts about 1,5 hours and you'll even ride past some cave paintings here and there. The longer (and more expensive) tour tells you more about the caves' history. You'll even have the opportunity to visit an underground chapel from the French era.

236 BLOKARTING ON THE BEACH

NATURAL HIGH
Brouwersdam 22
Ouddorp
South Holland
+31 (0)18 772 39 00
natural-high.nl

Is it a sailboat or a souped up go-cart? Neither, it's a blokart! This form of land yachting was originally invented in New Zealand. In the Netherlands you can try it out at Natural High on the North Sea beaches. Tear along the Brouwersdam which connects South Holland with Zeeland. Book your blokart online or by phone.

Fun trips with
PUBLIC TRANSPORT

237 WHITE BIKES IN DE HOGE VELUWE

DE HOGE VELUWE
NATIONAL PARK
Otterlo/
Hoenderloo
Gelderland
0800 835 3628
hogeveluwe.nl

The free Witte Fietsen (white bikes) in the Hoge Veluwe National Park date from the sixties. At the time, the Provos – a slightly anarchistic group of social innovators – suggested making these free white bikes available to everyone in Amsterdam. Ultimately the project never materialised. In De Hoge Veluwe, however, these white bikes have proven the best way to get around the park and visit the museums since several decades already. The bikes are everywhere, so there is no need to lock them (nor can you lock them).

238 TRAIN FROM MAASTRICHT TO HEERLEN

Maastricht
and Heerlen
Limburg
ns.nl

The train winds its way through the hills of South Limburg and stops at Valkenburg station en route. The oldest station of the Netherlands is built from blocks of marl, for which the region is famous. The local train takes a little longer and stops at more picturesque stations such as Klimmen-Ransdaal and Houthem-Sint Gerlach, the last wooden station in the Netherlands, which is also a nice place to start your walk in the area around the Geul River.

239 THE BUS THAT RUNS ALONG AFSLUITDIJK

Alkmaar and Leeuwarden
North Holland/ Friesland
9292.nl

You'll find a lunchroom, a monument and a watchtower with a view of the Wadden Sea and the IJsselmeer in the middle of the 32-kilometre-long Afsluitdijk. This dike separates North Holland from Friesland. If you think it's only worth doing with a car, then think again. Bus 350 from Alkmaar to Leeuwarden stops here once every hour during its tour of what is the world's most famous dike according to some.

240 TRAIN FROM ALMERE TO LELYSTAD

Almere and Lelystad
Flevoland
ns.nl

The train from Almere Centrum to Lelystad Centrum passes through Oostvaardersplassen, a man-made nature area that was created following the reclamation of Flevoland in the fifties and sixties. It is a popular stopping place for migratory birds. You can spot the large grazers and even the odd fox from the train.

241 TRAIN FROM AMSTERDAM TO ZANDVOORT

Amsterdam and Zandvoort
North Holland
ns.nl

The first part of your journey will take you to Haarlem, on the oldest railway line of the Netherlands. Haarlem is also one of the country's most beautiful train stations. The scene at Amsterdam-Central in the film *Ocean's Eleven* was actually filmed here. After Haarlem, the train stops at Overveen, a picturesque small station from 1881, from where you can easily walk to the dunes of the Zuid-Kennemerland National Park. You can smell the sea at Zandvoort station.

BOAT TRIPS

to feel the wind in your hair

---

242 A BOAT TRIP THROUGH THE PORT OF ROTTERDAM

Europaweg 902
Tweede Maasvlakte
Rotterdam
South Holland
+31 (0)10 252 25 20
portofrotterdam.com/
nl/eropuit/futureland

The Tweede Maasvlakte (Second Maas Plain), the most recent expansion of Rotterdam's port, is easily explored by boat. The Fast Ferry (see *ret.nl*) from Hoek van Holland drops port workers off at various stops in the port area. But if you really want to get to know the port better, then take the boat with an audio guide from the FutureLand Maasvlakte Museum. En route, you will see ships that are as tall as the Empire State Building, that can transport up to 20.000 containers. You will only realise how big they really are, however, when you sail past them. You can often spot seals here too. On very windy days, a bus tour is a better alternative. Remember to bring some form of ID as the bus also passes through privately owned sites.

243 NDSM FERRY

Amsterdam
North Holland
gvb.nl

The ferry to Amsterdam's bustling NDSM wharf leaves from behind Central Station and offers a free sightseeing tour that lasts about one hour. The tour winds its way along the IJ, past old warehouses and industrial sites and the new Houthavens district. You also see some modern architecture including the city's Law Courts and the Eye film museum.

244 WATERBUS TO DORDRECHT AND KINDERDIJK

Erasmusbrug
[Centre]
Rotterdam
South Holland
waterbus.nl

Waterbus Line 20 sails from the Erasmus Bridge in Rotterdam all the way to Dordrecht. If you're up for it, you can even hop off at the famous mills in Kinderdijk. 15 of the 19 mills that were built here to pump away the water and keep the polders dry are still occupied. Buy a Waterbus day ticket to enjoy a discount on your museum admission, and which includes a visit of two of the mills. You can also explore Dordrecht with the Waterbus. But this lovely tour along the Nieuwe Maas River and 'de Noord' is already an attraction in itself.

245 TOUR OF THE OOSTERSCHELDE

Nieuwe
Havenweg 5
Burghsluis
Zeeland
+31 (0)6 53 53 52 97
ms-onrust.nl

Zeeland was famous for its many ferries long before most of the islands were connected by roads. There are still plenty of ferries that sail in the summertime and you can also take your bike on board. The *MS Onrust* sails throughout the year, including in winter, and also offers tours of the Oosterschelde, the largest national park in the Netherlands. En route you can spot seals, porpoises (if you're lucky), plenty of waders and birds on the mudflats, and enjoy some stunning panoramic views. They also organise special evening tours or a mussel trip.

246 STAVOREN – ENKHUIZEN FERRY

Port of Stavoren
Port of Enkhuizen
Friesland/
North Holland
+31 (0)228 32 66 67
veerboot.info

Stavoren is the oldest city in Friesland and a popular stop for pleasure boats. The Lady of Stavoren still looks out over the water at the entrance to the port. According to a local legend, this rich merchant woman tossed her gold ring into the sea. The Stavoren-Enkhuizen ferry sails from April to October and will take you from one province to the other, across the IJsselmeer. You will be served coffee and cake on board and you can even take your bike with you (no cars however). You can easily get to Stavoren or Enkhuizen by train.

246 **PORT OF ENKHUIZEN**

Nature and wildlife
WALKS

247 DWINGELDERVELD

DWINGELDERVELD
NATIONAL PARK
Ruinen
Drenthe
staatsbosbeheer.nl

You have to tend the heath otherwise it will become overgrown with grasses, shrubs and trees in no time at all. That is why you may run into a shepherd and his flock of sheep on the heath now and then. The sheep ensure that you can continue to enjoy the lovely purple plants that flower every year in August. Dwingelderveld is a beautiful, large nature area in the north of Drenthe, with heath, sand drifts and plenty of fens, far removed from the busy city. You can find various signposted hiking trails on the website of Staatsbosbeheer.

248 A WALK ACROSS THE MUDFLATS

WADDEN SEA AREA
North Holland/
Friesland/
Groningen
vrijewadlopers.nl

You should take a walk across the mudflats at least once in your life. You won't get any closer to nature than this, when standing on a temporarily exposed spit of land, while the mud sucks up your boots, in the knowledge that you have to get out on time because the tide is turning. You can only walk on the mudflats with a guide, because the tide, wind speed and wind direction are all factors you must take into account during your walk. De Vrije Wadlopers organise walks with small groups in various locations along the Wadden Sea.

249 VELUWEZOOM

Rheden
Gelderland

While the De Veluwezoom is not as well-known as the larger De Hoge Veluwe National Park, it is just as beautiful nonetheless. And secretly, we also think it's more diverse: with lush, open, hilly heaths, old deciduous forests and stunning panoramic views. Here you can also find the Posbank, a vegetated, 90-metre-high moraine, which offers views of the surrounding area. From Rheden station, it's just a short walk to the visitor centre of the Veluwezoom National Park, where you can also rent bikes. There are several signposted hiking trails, each approximately 10 kilometres long, which start from various locations in the park.

250 RHOONSE GRIENDEN

Rhoon
South Holland
wandelzoekpagina.nl

The 'jungle' of South Holland is just a few metro stops from Rotterdam. The willow forests at Rhoon – which are called *grienden* – were previously used as a source for willow wood. This typical Dutch naturalised landscape has been left to go wild and is doing exactly that. Take a walk along Oude Maas, along densely vegetated trails, unwind on the golf course or sip an energising cup of coffee at Rhoon Castle. The Groene Wissel walk in this area is really lovely. The website features some lovely walking tours through the area.

251 NAARDERMEER

Naarden
North Holland
natuur
monumenten.nl

Naardermeer is one of the most beautiful nature areas of the Netherlands. In 1906, it was the first nature area to be listed as a protected nature area by Natuurmonumenten, a body that was specifically established for this purpose. Naardermeer was at risk of becoming a landfill for Amsterdam. Author, lecturer and nature lover Jac. P. Thijsse was one of the many people who protested against this development. Naardermeer is a very large lake. But the Laarzenpad trail is a great place to walk, with plenty of birdwatching huts and fun walkways. The website has a more detailed map of the complete 6,5-kilometre Laarzenpad trail.

252 LOONSE EN DRUNENSE DUINEN

DE LOONSE EN
DRUNENSE DUINEN
NATIONAL PARK
North Brabant
np-deloonseen
drunenseduinen.nl

You'd usually expect to find dunes at the seaside. But there are plenty of impressive sand drifts in various locations in the Netherlands. The most beautiful ones are the dunes at Loon and Drunen. This area is sometimes also called the 'Brabant Sahara'. The landscape here is much more varied than in North Africa however, with forests, heaths and plenty of places to quench your thirst in the many bars and pubs around the national park. The hiking trails are signposted, but you can also find a map online at *natuurmonumenten.nl*.

252 LOONSE EN DRUNENSE DUINEN

ARCEN CASTLE GARDENS

LANDSCAPES ⏏

The most beautiful **B E A C H E S**

253 **WESTKAPELLE**

Westkapelle
Zeeland
westkapelle.com

The 12-kilometre-long sandy beach of Westkapelle is situated on the westernmost tip of the Zeeland island of Walcheren. The ships from and to the Westerschelde sail by, close to the beach. Find a spot at one of the beach pavilions and watch the sun set while you tuck into some tasty Zeeland mussels.

254 **SCHOORL AAN ZEE**

Schoorl
North Holland
duindorpschoorl.nl

You won't find overflowing parking lots and boulevards full of tourist shops or loud cafes and restaurants in Schoorl aan Zee because you can only get to the beach on foot or by bike. The 5-kilometre hiking and cycling trails wind their way through the country's highest dunes. A contrast with the rest of the coast of North Holland.

255 **ROCKANJE**

Rockanje
South Holland
rockanjeaanzee.com

A beach which is very popular with families and the elderly because of the lack of large waves. The sandbanks break the waves and the current, and the sea becomes only gradually deeper. The Groene Punt nature area is located to the north, towards the Tweede Maasvlakte (Second Maas Plain) where the beach curves around the bend. At low tide, you can see bunkers from World War II here.

257 CADZAND-BAD

256 DE BALG

De Balg
Schiermonnikoog
Friesland

You expect to run into Mad Max any moment here. The Balg, the easternmost beach of Schiermonnikoog, is vast and deserted. It is claimed that this is Europe's widest beach, although there are other beaches vying for the title. At low tide, the easternmost tip of the island is revealed. You can regularly find seals relaxing on the sandbanks.

257 CADZAND-BAD

Cadzand
Zeeland
cadzand.org

In recent years, Cadzand-Bad has changed substantially, in a bid to make this a more upmarket seaside resort. Unfortunately, the ban on building along the coast was lifted, even though this is a no-go in much of the Netherlands. The southernmost beach of Zeeland has retained its charm however. And it's still a good place to go hunting for fossil shark's teeth.

Magnificent
COUNTRY ESTATES

258 DOORN HOUSE

Langbroeker-
weg 10
Doorn
Utrecht
+31 (0)343 42 10 20
huisdoorn.nl

Wilhelm II, Germany's last kaiser, wanted to emigrate to the Netherlands after Germany lost World War I. The Netherlands, which were neutral, were uncertain how to respond to this request. Nonetheless, Wilhelm purchased the Doorn country house, in the present-day Utrechtse Heuvelrug National Park. He had 59 train cars of furniture transferred here from his German castles. The beautifully preserved interior gives a good idea of how people lived in those days. Outside you can find monumental trees, a rose garden,

258 **DOORN HOUSE**

and the woodcutting spot where Wilhelm II liked to work daily. He lived there until his death in 1941. And because the German monarchy has not been restored, he is still buried here. The mausoleum is closed, but you can still see his sarcophagus, through the bars and the stained glass.

259 BOUVIGNE

Bouvignelaan 5
Breda
North Brabant
+31 (0)76 564 10 60
landgoedbouvigne.nl

Bouvigne Castle, as we know it today, dates from the early 17th century and is situated on the edge of Mastbos and Markdal, an old Dutch landscape with pastures, brooks and reed belts, with plenty of hiking and cycling trails. The three gardens around the castle were designed in the early 20th century, according to the prevailing English, German and French garden styles. You can only visit the castle on special occasions but the gardens are open on working days, from 8 am until 5 pm, through the adjoining offices of the water board.

260 FRAEYLEMABORG

Hoofdweg 30
Slochteren
Groningen
+31 (0)598 42 15 68
fraeylemaborg.nl

Slochteren is famous because of the huge natural gas field that was discovered here in the late fifties. But the village existed long before, as evidenced by the 18th-century Fraeylemaborg (a *borg* is a kind of castle typical to the province of Groningen). The *borg* has a historical interior, with classic furniture, old toys and a few paintings by Mesdag. The building was recently renovated in a sustainable way. The huge, 23-hectare landscape garden is dotted with so-called follies, a bunch of whimsical and seemingly useless art objects.

261 ROSENDAEL CASTLE

Rosendael 1
Rozendaal
Gelderland
+31 (0)26 364 46 45
rosendael.glk.nl

Watch out when you walk across the mosaic floor of the fountain in the park garden of medieval Rosendael Castle because now and then water suddenly squirts up out of it. These surprising fountains are very popular again and are often used by the designers of new city squares. Rosendael Castle has had such fountains since 1732, where they are part of the exuberant shell gallery by architect Daniel Marot.

262 TWICKEL COUNTRY ESTATE

Twickelerlaan 7
Ambt Delden
Overijssel
+31 (0)74 376 10 20
twickel.nl

The country estate around Twickel Castle, which is still occupied today, covers a surface area of 4400 hectares and has plenty of ornamental and cottage gardens as well as 150 historic farms. A great place to explore the characteristic half-open landscape of Twente. The steep pedestrian bridge, which runs over the ring road, restored the historic walking trail between the country estate and the nearby medieval village of Delden.

263 THE SHELL CAVE OF BORG NIENOORD

Nienoord 20
Leek
Groningen
+31 (0)594 51 22 30
landgoednienoord.nl

This shell cave, which dates from 1700, in the garden of Borg Nienoord is the last original example of its kind in the Netherlands. Legend has it that this shell cave has a rather dramatic origin. The maid Geeske was very curious about the treasures that the lady of the manor kept in her garden shed. She decided to take a peek but was caught by the count. He decided to lock her up in the garden shed in lieu of punishment, where she was forced to decorate the walls with shells. It took her 20 years. Upon her release, she was so shocked at her mirror image that she dropped dead on the spot.

PARKS

for the perfect day out

---

264 PARK GRAVENRODE

Landgraaf
Limburg

Located in a former mining area between Landgraaf en Kerkrade, Park Gravenrode comprises several touristic attractions, including two castles, a zoo, a botanical garden and a discovery museum about our planet, science and technology. A must-do is climbing the largest stairs in the Netherlands that will take you to the top of the Wilhelminaberg (where you'll also find a ski slope). Part of this park are the gardens of Mondo Verde.

265 MÁXIMA PARK

Máximapark
Utrecht
maximapark.nl

Everything is big in the Utrecht new-build district of Leidsche Rijn. It is said that this district is home to as many people as the population of the town of Leeuwarden. The new 300-hectare city park is just as large as the old city centre of Utrecht. It's a great place to walk and bike. The highlights are the lush Butterfly Garden, which was designed by the landscape architect Piet Oudolf, and the Maximus brewery where you can sample a local beer, which is brewed with hops from the park.

266 SONSBEEK PARK

Park Sonsbeek
Arnhem
Gelderland
sonsbeek.nl

Sections of the hilly Sonsbeek Park, which was once a privately owned country estate, are developed like an English landscape garden. The cherry on the cake is the Swiss-style waterfall. Another part of the park is populated with old beech trees. You can enjoy amazing views of the landscape around Arnhem from the belvedere or viewpoint on the 70-metre-high Ruyterenberg.

267 DAKPARK

Vierhavenstraat
(between Marconi-
plein and
Hudsonplein)
[West]
Rotterdam
South Holland
dakparkrotterdam.nl

This roof park on top of a kilometre-long stretch of shops opened in 2014. It is a welcome addition to an area that is very much characterised by concrete and cars. It's also a good way of capturing excess rainwater. The park is managed by the locals. The water steps are especially busy in the summer months, with children from the diverse neighbourhood of Rotterdam-West.

268 HAARLEMMERHOUT

Haarlemmerhout
Haarlem
North Holland

The Haarlemmerhout city forest has a long history as a recreational green space. It dates from the Middle Ages although the eastern section of the park is indicative of 19th-century styles, when the park was redeveloped. You can also see a deer camp here and there are plenty of pubs and cafes in green surroundings. The sections to the west of the road are wilder and attract a lot of vegetation and animals.

Instagrammable
GARDENS

269 ARCEN CASTLE GARDENS

Lingsforterweg 26
Arcen
Limburg
+31 (0)77 473 60 10
kasteeltuinen.nl

This beautiful garden, behind Arcen Castle, was designed and developed in 1988, by the Limburgs Landschap Foundation. It originally started out as a rose garden, because Limburg has plenty of rose growers. The garden now encompasses 21 different gardens, including small show gardens, which were designed to inspire visitors before the Internet and Pinterest. The oriental water gardens, with bamboo

269 ARCEN CASTLE GARDENS

paths, ponds with koi carp, rockeries, Japanese maples and the inevitable Buddha sculptures are especially worthwhile. You can find plenty of other exotic species in the large greenhouse, including tall fig trees and banana plants, birds of paradise and passion flowers. You may even run into storks and flamingos here. The garden is closed in the winter months, but you can easily spend a whole day here during the other seasons.

270 TROMPENBURG GARDENS & ARBORETUM

Honingerdijk 86
[East]
Rotterdam
South Holland
+31 (0)10 233 01 66
trompenburg.nl

It's easy to see why so many newly-weds choose this place for their wedding photos: Trompenburg's gardens provide a stunning setting, with brooks and ponds, small bridges, rhododendron bushes, hostas and beautiful beech trees with red and brown leaves. This is a lovely place to take a walk in lush green surroundings and get away from the bustling city. The cactus greenhouse and the *pinetum* (small pine forest) are especially quiet.

271 PRINSENTUIN

Turfsingel 43
Groningen

This hidden gem in the city centre of Groningen is situated just behind the Martini Tower. The renaissance garden was built in 1626 for the Princes of Nassau who resided at Prinsenhof. The romantic rose and herb garden with vistas and hedges, and a working solar dial above the gate are still very popular. The garden was almost lost however. In the 19th century, they built a morgue and stables here. Prinsentuin has since been restored to its former glory.

272 VERBORGEN STADSTUIN ZWOLLE

Assendorper-
straat 178
Zwolle
Overijssel
+31 (0)38 422 05 64
tuinharrypierik.nl

In the early eighties, Harry Pierik's garden was a derelict field, with rusty old iron, abandoned mattresses and plastic. This hidden city garden has since been transformed into a lush, magical dream garden, where you can lose yourself like Alice in Wonderland. As you walk through it, you will be sucked into the garden, with the changing perspectives along the hilly trails. You can only visit this private garden on appointment or during the open garden weekends.

273 HEEMTUIN RUCPHEN

Baanvelden 12
Rucphen
North Brabant
+31 (0)165 34 30 14
heemtuinrucphen.nl

The heritage garden was created by the founding father of nature preservation and nature education in the Netherlands, Jac. P. Thijsse. It was designed to teach people about indigenous plants and animals. One of the most beautiful heritage gardens is located in Rucphen in Brabant, where you can explore 19 different local habitats, from heath to fens and river valleys. The garden, which is also a sheltered workplace, is renowned for its wildflowers and also had a seedling of the Anne Frank tree. This was the chestnut tree that Anne Frank could see from the Secret Annex and which she wrote about.

274 DE DREIJEN BOTANIC GARDEN

Arboretumlaan 4
Wageningen
Gelderland
+31 (0)317 46 77 20
hetdepot.nl

Wageningen's botanic garden was designed as an educational tool for the Rijkstuinbouwschool, the predecessor of Wageningen University. The teacher and landscape architect Leonard Springer designed this English landscape garden, and planted special trees, like the giant mammoth tree, the silk tree with its pretty pink blossoms and the Chinese tupelo tree with its vibrant red blooms. The garden also has a nice sculpture gallery, called the Depot.

GET YOUR FEET WET
to experience nature

275 VERDRONKEN LAND VAN SAEFTINGHE

Emmaweg 4
Nieuw-Namen
Zeeland
+31 (0)114 63 31 10
saeftinghe.eu

The sea made way for polders. And now Saeftinghe is flooded again. The agricultural land, the villages and even the castle have been returned to nature and now lie dormant under the water. Saeftinghe is located in the Westerschelde estuary and is a brackish marshland. The tides rise very fast here because of the many channels and gullies. Here freshwater and saltwater merge. The mudflats and salt marshes are a very nutrient-rich habitat, attracting up to 200 different bird species. You can take a walk along the dike, starting from the visitor centre (which is closed in the winter months). If you want to walk deeper into Saeftinghe, we recommend booking a guided walk.

276 DE BIESBOSCH

Werkendam/
Drimmelen/
Dordrecht
North Brabant/
South Holland
np-debiesbosch.nl

You can explore De Biesbosch on foot or by bike. But the best experience is from the water, in a canoe or an electric boat. This vast nature area connects South Holland and North Brabant. It used to be a popular area with fishermen and cutters of reeds, rushes and wicker. During World War II, you could find people hiding in here, as well as resistance fighters and smugglers. Nowadays it's home to unique animal species such as the beaver (look for signs of gnawing along the banks or droppings on the river bed) and the bald eagle.

275 VERDRONKEN LAND VAN SAEFTINGHE

277 DE GROOTE PEEL

Moostdijk 15
Ospel
Limburg
+31 (0)495 64 14 97
staatsbosbeheer.nl

The Groote Peel peat moor is situated on the border between Brabant and Limburg. This marshy nature area has plenty of boardwalks from where you can spot unique bird species, such as the black-necked grebe. Enjoy the expansive views, and travel back in time to the era of the first peat cutters. The De Pelen visitor centre is a good place to start your visit.

278 DE ALDE FEANEN

Koaidyk 8-A
Earnewâld
Friesland
+31 (0)511 53 96 18
np-aldefeanen.nl

Here you can spot the bittern, the bearded reedling, the marsh harrier and the bluethroat. The Alde Feanen (old fens) is an old lowland moor, where people used to harvest peat, but which gradually came to be flooded. Now it is one of the largest marshes in Western Europe with large ponds and reed beds. Take a walk or visit it with a boat and use one of the many birdwatching huts to get a better view of the bird population.

279 LAUWERSMEER

De Rug 1
Lauwersoog
Groningen
+31 (0)519 34 51 45
np-lauwersmeer.nl

After the dam was built here, a stunning nature area flourished on the former sea bed, which is now one of the Netherlands' most populated bird reserves. Like in the Biesbosch, you may spot a bald eagle here, as well as stilts, the red-necked phalarope and the pectoral sandpiper. This is an important stopping place during the trek from the Arctic to Africa, which is why you can spot so many special species here. Lauwersmeer is also a Dark Sky Park, where you can still see the stars at night. This is quite unique, as the Netherlands is known for its light pollution.

BRAM EN AAGIE

SHOPPING 🔒

Inspiring
BOOKSHOPS

280 DOMINICANEN

Dominicaner-
kerkstraat 1
Maastricht
Limburg
+31 (0)43 410 00 10
*boekhandel
dominicanen.nl*

This bookshop is one of the most impressive shops in its genre, and is located in a 700-year-old Gothic Dominican church. There are 17th-century frescos on the ceilings of the church's vaults and the mural of St. Thomas Aquinas from 1337 is said to be one of the oldest portrayals of this saint in Europe. During the restoration in 2006, a huge walk-in book cabinet, with several floors, was added, increasing the shop's floor area and offering amazing views of the church interior.

280 DOMINICANEN

281 DONNER

Coolsingel 129
[Centre]
Rotterdam
South Holland
+31 (0)10 413 20 70
donner.nl

Rotterdam's largest bookshop has experienced a few turbulent years. The shop was established in 1912 by the alderman J.H. Donner, only to be completely destroyed on 14 May 1940 when the Germans bombed the city. It was rebuilt and relocated several times. In 2006, a large chain acquired Donner, selling it to another chain, that went bankrupt in 2014, threatening to take several reputable bookshops down with it. Donner was saved by 2000 book lovers, who contributed to the crowdfunding campaign and formed a cooperative. Donner is housed in a former bank in Coolsingel, the first large construction project after the destruction of May 1940. The stained-glass window in the stairwell by glass artist Andries Copier has been restored to its former glory after a major renovation.

282 WATERSTONES

Kalverstraat 152
Amsterdam
[Centre]
North Holland
+31 (0)20 638 38 21
waterstones.com

Stepping into Waterstones is like setting foot in a nice old library, albeit one with personal tips from the shop's employees on notes among the books. The shop is located in a monumental building by the Dutch architect H.P. Berlage, which gives out onto the Spui. The city's book square is also famous for its weekly book market on Fridays.

283 THE AMERICAN BOOK CENTER

Spui 12
[Centre]
Amsterdam
North Holland
+31 (0)20 625 55 37
abc.nl

The American Book Center's unrivalled selection of English literature, graphic novels and magazines is not the only reason why you should visit this bookshop. 'ABC', which is located in the Spui, where you'll find two other bookshops, is also the place where Amsterdam's book lovers meet. Keep an eye on their website as they organise plenty of events in Amsterdam and at their smaller branch in The Hague (Lange Poten 23).

284 BROESE

Oudegracht 112-b
Utrecht
+31 (0)30 233 52 00
broese.nl

Broese is the most iconic bookshop in Utrecht's city centre, with a nice selection of fiction and non-fiction. In 2020, after 40 years at the Stadhuis-brug, the shop moved a little further down the Oudegracht canal, into the listed art deco building that used to be the city's post office. It was renovated, repurposed and now houses the city library, some shops, and a food market.

285 DE VRIES VAN STOCKUM

Gedempte Oude
Gracht 27
Haarlem
North Holland
+31 (0)23 531 94 58
devriesboeken.nl

In the past 100 years, this book treasury has grown to its current size, encompassing five shopfronts. De Vries has the most comprehensive selection of books in Haarlem and possibly even the Netherlands. You can spend hours browsing this shop and even sit down with a book at the reading table or near the fireplace.

286 VAN PIERE

Nieuwe
Emmasingel 48
Eindhoven
North Brabant
+31 (0)40 249 20 02
vanpiere.nl

Van Piere has been supplying the people of
Eindhoven with good literature since 1848. The
books are stacked right up to the ceiling here,
and if seeing all that paper makes you thirsty,
then pop into Coffee Lovers for a cappuccino or
a latte. Van Piere organises several events, including
history cafes and 'Boekie Nights' (literary talk shows
with music).

287 VAN DER MEER

De Keuvel 1
Noordwijk
South Holland
+31 (0)71 361 30 73
*boekhandel
vandermeer.nl*

A bookshop that won the 'Best Bookseller' award
twice has to have some kind of wow factor. You'll
immediately understand why when you see the
interior and browse their amazing collection. They
have a bar made of books, music instruments are
strewn everywhere (on the floor, the ceiling, the
walls) and they have plenty of comfy leather club
chairs where you can sit down and read. Every
Thursday they cook from a cookbook, after which
you can share what you've cooked at the long table.

288 VAN DER VELDE

Nieuwestad 57-59
Leeuwarden
Friesland
+31 (0)58 213 23 60
*boekhandel
vandervelde.nl*

Van der Velde has several shops in the north
of the country but it all started in Leeuwarden
in 1892. Nowadays this bookshop consists of
a modern shop with an antiquarian bookshop
with three floors of secondhand books next door,
in a monumental building. They regularly exhibit
art in the Slauerhoff courtyard, where they also
host poetry readings and music concerts.

292 WAANDERS IN DE BROEREN

289 DE DRVKKERY

Markt 51
Middelburg
Zeeland
+31 (0)118 88 68 86
de-drvkkery.nl

De Drvkkery is easy to recognise because of its striking glass façade. This shop stocks more titles (50.000!) than there are inhabitants in Middelburg. What's more, they also have a nice collection of music, national and international newspapers and magazines. The brasserie is a great place for breakfast. On Thursday evenings, they also serve a (vegetarian or other) three-course dinner. Jan de Vlieger, the current owner, was a vicar until he became a bookseller in 2017. He described De Drvkkery as follows in an interview: "It's like a horizon, that unfolds before you".

290 PAAGMAN

Frederik
Hendriklaan 217
The Hague
South Holland
+31 (0)88 338 38 38
paagman.nl

The Paagman family company has various shops in The Hague but the oldest one is located in the city's shopping street, in Frederik Hendriklaan (or 'de Fred' as the locals call it). Writers regularly visit this 'living room in the Statenkwartier'. Pop into Villa Paagman, the children's bookshop, and the Kicking Horse Café for coffee or lunch.

291 DEN BOER

Laanstraat 67-69
Baarn
Utrecht
+31 (0)35 542 68 51
denboer.nl

Time seems to have stopped in this book temple although the selection is continuously updated. The warm, wood-panelled interior still looks like it did in 1887, when the first bookshop opened here in this monumental art nouveau building. From 1900 onwards, Hendrik Jacobus den Boer, ran the bookshop with his wife Dina Breijer, a German teacher, who also produced the first translation of Herman Hesse's *Siddharta*.

292 WAANDERS IN DE BROEREN

Achter de
Broeren 1-3
Zwolle
Overijssel
+31 (0)38 421 53 92
waanders
indebroeren.nl

Another church, in the medieval fortified city of Zwolle, that was converted into a book lover's haven. Three open floors were added during the radical renovation of the 15th-century Broeren church, retaining the serenity and majesty of this white church interior.

Superb
MUSEUM SHOPS

293 DE KUNSTHAL

MUSEUMPARK
Westzeedijk 341
[Centre]
Rotterdam
South Holland
+31 (0)10 440 03 00
kunsthalshop.nl

Rotterdam's Kunsthal was the first of its kind in the Netherlands when it opened in the early nineties: it has 33.000 square metres of exhibition space but no collection of its own. The centre organises between 20 and 30 temporary exhibitions here every year, and the selection in the museum shop reflects this. The shop is located between the entrance and the restaurant, in an iconic building by Rotterdam architect Rem Koolhaas.

294 RIJKSMUSEUM

Museumstraat 1
[Museum Quarter]
Amsterdam
North Holland
+31 (0)20 674 70 00
rijksmuseumshop.nl

The Rijksmuseum is in a league of its own. Its collection includes some of the most famous works from the Dutch Golden Age and plenty of Asian art. The museum shop has an amazing selection of goodies including socks with Rembrandt's *The Night Watch*, as well as home accessories and replicas of famous works. The 'Rijks' runs the Museum Shop in Museumplein together with the nearby Van Gogh Museum.

295 BONNEFANTEN-MUSEUM

Avenue
Céramique 250
Maastricht
Limburg
+31 (0)43 329 01 11
bonnefanten.nl

You don't need to buy a ticket to visit the shop of the Bonnefantenmuseum, which stocks a good selection of art books and accessories. But you really should visit this beautifully located building by Aldo Rossi with its good collection of old and modern art. The Bonnefantenmuseum regularly hosts sensational exhibitions by acclaimed artists such as Grayson Perry, Melanie Bonajo or David Lynch.

296 STEDELIJK MUSEUM

Museumplein 10
[Museum Quarter]
Amsterdam
North Holland
+31 (0)20 573 29 11
stedelijk.nl

Not everyone took a shining to the striking new-build, with which the Stedelijk Museum more than doubled its exhibition space a few years ago. The locals soon took to calling it 'the bath tub'. Regardless of what you think of it, the 'Stedelijk' is still a great museum, where you can see art and design masterpieces of the 20th and 21st century. The museum shop stocks a wide range of books on art, design and photography.

297 MUSEUM VOORLINDEN

Buurtweg 90
Wassenaar
South Holland
+31 (0)70 512 16 60
voorlinden.nl

The Voorlinden shop is almost as much fun as the museum itself. It's a great place to shop for gifts or a little memento of your visit, that stocks an extensive collection of books and design objects.

298 GRONINGER MUSEUM

Museumeiland 1
Groningen
+31 (0)50 366 65 55
groningermuseum.nl

The unique post-modern building of the Groninger Museum is an attraction in itself, with its large golden tower and colourful, overhanging pavilions. The Italian architect Alessandro Mendini designed a museum that allowed various designers to create pavilions to exhibit the museum's diverse collection (from archaeology and painting to design). The selection of items in the colourful museum shop, which was designed by Groningen-based Vorm Martini, is just as eclectic as the building and the collection.

299 CENTRAAL MUSEUM

Agnietenstraat 1
Utrecht
+31 (0)30 236 23 49
centraalmuseum.nl

The Centraal Museum has something for everyone, including the remnants of a Viking ship, furniture by Rietveld and striking works by the renaissance artist Jan van Scorel, the magical realist Pyke Koch and the surrealist Joop Moesman. The Nijntje Museum on the opposite of the street is very popular with children. The museum shop stocks a wide range of books and gadgets that refer to the temporary exhibitions and plenty of gadgets featuring Dick Bruna's world-famous white bunny rabbit.

Unique **ANTIQUE** and **VINTAGE** shops

300 VAN LEEST ANTIQUES

Mariaplaats 45
Utrecht
+31 (0)6 547 77 074
vanleestantiques.com

Anatomical models, old medical instruments, telescopes and sundials: Van Leest Antiques has the most amazing collection, which is even better than the collections of some science museums. This shop in the centre of Utrecht specialises in medical and scientific instruments. The owner describes himself as a 'tandiquair': he trained and worked as a dentist (tandarts) but is really passionate about antiques.

301 DE MUSEUM-WINKEL

Van Welderen-
straat 114
Nijmegen
Gelderland
+31 (0)24 360 05 06
*demuseum
winkel.com*

Occasionally De Museumwinkel in Nijmegen makes the headlines. For example, when they sold a 19th-century shrunken human head from the Amazon. Fortunately you can also find less grizzly items here, although their collection of stuffed animals is difficult to ignore. Other items on sale include fossils, minerals and other gems for a well-stocked cabinet of curiosities.

302 **PANDORA**

Wijnstraat 82-86
Dordrecht
South Holland
+31 (0)78 613 50 30
pandora-dordt.eu

Housed in a monumental 18th-century monument once the site of the city's theatre, Pandora is a veritable treasure trove. It's fun to browse the stacks of books, LPs, antiques, knickknacks and furniture. Nearby is 'little brother' Pandorus (Boomstraat 17) comprising an additional three storeys of vintage and retro-items.

300 VAN LEEST ANTIQUES

303 FITZROY & EVEREST GENTLEMEN'S ANTIQUES

Vredehofstraat 54-B
[East]
Rotterdam
South Holland
+31 (0)10 411 88 01
fitzroy-everest.nl

A leather chest from the twenties, antique golf clubs or an old globe. Gentlemen will find plenty of items to their taste at this antiques store in the upmarket Rotterdam neighbourhood of Kralingen. The owner Olivier van Schaik has a soft spot for objects from the twenties and thirties, and the craftsmanship, robust materials and beautiful finish of this period.

304 'T ALLEGAARTJE

Harlingerweg 1
Franeker
Friesland
+31 (0)6 15 50 69 61
allegaartje
franeker.nl

There is no rhyme or reason to the set-up here. Everything is stacked in two large spaces, from floor to ceiling. If you're not one to be dissuaded by this visual assault, then this is the place to go on a treasure hunt because 't Allegaartje sells anything from old school maps to vintage tins and furniture. Vintage done right.

SPECIALITY SHOPS

for special finds

---

305 BRAM EN AAGIE

Raadhuisstraat 21
Graft
North Holland
+31 (0)6 53 31 76 09
bramenaagie.nl

As you cycle through the Beemster, the shop of Bram en Aagie provides a welcome distraction. (Since 1890!), you can buy all kinds of old-fashioned sweets, including cinnamon sticks, liquorice and syrup candy in what is the 'tiniest candy shop in the Netherlands'. In fact you can barely stand up here. The shop has been in hands of the same family for many years. Grandson Jaap Klaver now runs it.

306 NEVERNEVERLAND

Oudegracht 202
Utrecht
+31 (0)30 233 22 93
neverneverland
utrecht.nl

NeverNeverland proves that sitting around a table and playing a board game has lost none of its appeal despite the popularity of online games. Here you can score the latest board games, card games and puzzles, as well as lots of classics and parts. They give great advice and you can even test (some of the) games at the table in the shop.

307 AFFAIRE D'EAU

Haarlemmer-
dijk 150
[Centre]
Amsterdam
North Holland
+31 (0)20 422 04 11
affairedeau.com

It all started with a wonderful collection of antique bath tubs from a French spa resort hotel. Now, more than 30 years later, Affaire d'Eau is a well-established seller of antique sanitary ware, as well as decorative items such as Christmas decorations, botanical scale models, but also perfumes and shower gels.

308 DE REFTER

Nieuwland-
straat 23-25
Tilburg
North Brabant
+31 (0)13 543 12 29
refter.nl

A *refter* is the Dutch word for a refectory, where monks eat. This shop specialises in furniture from convents and monasteries. So what can you find here? Plenty of thick, leather-bound books, as well as statues of saints, crockery, glassware, cabinets and stunning prints.

309 HET KLAVERBLAD

Hogewoerd 15
Leiden
South Holland
+31 (0)71 513 36 55
hetklaverblad.com

This is the oldest coffee and tea shop of the Netherlands, where you can still spot the initials of the Dutch East India Company on the façade, and where tea is still sold in tea caddies. The shop was established in 1769. When you step inside, it feels like you've just embarked on a journey back in time.

310 WERELDWIJVEN ATELIERS

Voorstraat 178
Dordrecht
South Holland
+31 (0)78 613 63 07
wereldwijven ateliers.nl

Here you can shop for the most unique cushions, shawls, plaids and bags, which are sewn in their own workshop by *Wereldwijven,* or women from different cultural and ethnic backgrounds. Founder Jolanda Branderhorst thought it was rather strange that fashion designers travel to distant countries to produce their designs, when there is so much creative and artisan expertise available closer to home. They also regularly host exhibitions and performances.

DE KOP VAN 'T LAND

FOOD 🍴

Unusual locations for a
SNACK

---

311 SMICKEL-INN 'BALKON VAN EUROPA'

Slag Maasmond 10
Tweede Maasvlakte
Rotterdam
South Holland
+31 (0)6 57 79 12 10

Drive and just when you think you're there, it's just a little further. The Balkon van Europa snack bar is at the outermost tip of the Tweede Maasvlakte, approximately 60 kilometre from the centre of Rotterdam, tucked away among the wind turbines. And yet it's like setting foot in a cosy pub. Port workers, surfers, boat spotters and the odd tourist gaze at the immense containerships that sail up Nieuwe Waterweg. On sunny days, you can see The Hague on the horizon. There's a tiny strip of beach where you can bathe although there are also some larger sandy beaches along the route.

312 DE STAL

Darwinweg 1
Leiden
South Holland
+31 (0)71 523 05 80
destal.nu

Herman the bull was a world first when he was born in 1990, as the first genetically modified bovine ever. A human protein was added to his DNA causing massive protests, and many people even suggested that Herman be put down. Ultimately the then Agriculture Minister ordered that Herman should be castrated and live the rest of his living days in a stable at the University of Leiden's current Bio Science Park. Many years later, the stable was turned into a restaurant for people who live or study nearby. And Herman? He died, was stuffed, and is displayed in the Naturalis Museum of Natural History.

313 TERRAS OVERWIJK

Laaksum 7
Warns
Friesland
+31 (0)514 68 22 69

Laaksum calls itself the smallest port of the Netherlands, and even Europe. There's not much else to see than a few boats and a casual cafe with a large terrace. But it's a nice pitstop as you tour the southwest of Friesland and a great place to stop for a decent snack, some fish and chips, coffee and cake or a sunset drink. Experience the vast expanse of the IJsselmeer from the terrace. It's like standing at the edge of the world.

314 BRASSERIE HOFFMANNI

Lage Kanaal-
dijk 115
Maastricht
Limburg
+31 (0)6 43 78 24 38
bistrohoffmanni.nl

No, it's not Yellowstone National Park, although you may be forgiven for thinking so when you spot the azure blue water amidst the carved out white rocks. They mined marl here for over 100 years in the ENCI quarry. In 2018, operation closed down and the land is now gradually being returned to nature. Space is being created for businesses and leisure on the fringe of the site. Brasserie Hoffmanni, near the old industrial buildings, was one of the first to move in. Walk down from Sint-Pietersberg along the staircase in Luikerweg. If you've come by car, then follow the Maasboulevard and take the Châlet d'n Observant exit.

313 TERRAS OVERWIJK

315 JANS AAN ZEE

Hoogh Plaetweg 1
Vrouwenpolder
Zeeland
+31 (0)6 20 31 60 26
jansaanzee.nl

The island of Neeltje Jans, halfway along the Oosterscheldekering, has become synonymous for this section of the Delta Works, which protect Zeeland from the water during storms. You'll find snack bar Jans aan Zee on the west side of the road. Once a year, these dams feature as a parcours for the annual NK Tegenwindfietsen (headwind cycling championships): an 8,5-kilometre race that's organised at a minimum of wind force 7. Only bikes with backpedal brakes and without gears are allowed.

316 'T ZIELHOES

Zijlweg 4
Usquert
Groningen
+31 (0)595 42 30 58
zielhoes.nl

Noordpolderzijl, in Usquert has the smallest seaport in the Netherlands. You'll find 't Zielhoes at the foot of the dike, in the former lock keeper's house. It exudes a timeless ambiance. Worn floorboards, rugs on the tables and a pot-bellied stove that is lit up as soon as temperatures drop. Outside, the terrace overlooks the flat, Groninger countryside and the sea. The menu is short but fulfilling. Think eggs sunny-side-up, a Dutch shrimp sandwich, fries or croquettes served on bread.

317 SNACKBAR DE PIER

Koningin Emma-
boulevard 11
Hoek van Holland
South Holland
+31 (0)174 38 47 97
snackbardepier.nl

In the forties, the German army built approximately 2000 bunkers in the region around Hoek van Holland to defend Rotterdam's port. One of these bunkers has now been converted into a chips shop. The counter is near the embrasure, from where the soldiers monitored the beach. In the summer months, the people on the beach and the locals wait in long queues for a serving of the local world-famous *raspatat* potatoes. Closer to the beach, you'll find a bunker with an Atlantikwall museum, which is open on weekends.

The best places for
FRESH FISH

---

318 SIMONIS AAN DE HAVEN

Visafslagweg 20
The Hague
South Holland
+31 (0)70 350 00 42
simonisvis.nl

You could call Simonis a fish dynasty. In 1880, grandfather Simonis opened an eel smokehouse in The Hague, and his descendants followed with several fish shops and stalls in and around The Hague. Their spacious location on the Scheveningen harbour opened in 1980. You can go there for *kibbeling* (fried fish), fresh herring or an oyster paired with a glass of wine, but also for an entire plate of *fruits de mer* or a salad.

319 VISSCHER SEAFOOD

Melkmarkt 32
Zwolle
Overijssel
+31 (0)38 423 49 27
visscherseafood
zwolle.nl

This large, well-lit place in the centre of the walled city of Zwolle has plenty of tables where you can sit and eat your catch from the shop. A herring, or do you prefer a platter of fried mussels or squid, chips and a salad?

320 HOKKAI KITCHEN

Egmondstraat 2
IJmuiden
North Holland
+31 (0)6 13 14 62 46
hokkaikitchen.nl

This Japanese *toko* is a well-kept secret, that is tucked away in a business park in IJmuiden. The chef used to work in a Michelin-starred Japanese restaurant in Amsterdam. As this eatery is practically in the fish market, all the ingredients he uses for his sushi and other dishes are as fresh as they get and partly dependent on what looked best when he went to the market in the morning.

321 PUUR ZEE

Van Ogtropweg 2
Wijk aan Zee
North Holland
+31 (0)251 37 43 04
puurzee.nl

Michelin-star chef Imko Binnerts opened a fish restaurant in the lovely 130-year-old Hotel Villa De Klughte. Not a long list of à la carte options. Instead up to seven courses, prepared by the chef using fresh, seasonal and mostly regional and organic ingredients. Plenty of German wines on the excellent wine list.

322 BRASSERIE VLUCHTHAVEN

Zijpe 1
Bruinisse
Zeeland
+31 (0)111 48 12 28
vluchthaven.com

The majority of the shellfish, fish and Oosterschelde lobsters that are served at this restaurant in the Zeeland 'mussel village' of Bruinisse are locally sourced. So they are super fresh and served in a casual ambience. On sunny days, you can sit on the outdoor terrace with a view of the water. Open from March until October.

REGIONAL PRODUCTS
you must taste

___

323 OYSTERS

OESTERIJ
Havendijk 12
Yerseke
Zeeland
+31 (0)113 760 400
oesterij.nl

Given that you're in the epicentre of the Dutch oyster trade, we can see how you'd be interested in sampling the goods. Dhooge, a family business, has a shop and a tasting room where you can sample this Zeeland delicacy. Zeeland oysters are mainly sourced from the Oosterschelde and Grevelingenmeer. Before being sold and consumed, the oysters spend some time 'relaxing' in the 19th-century oyster pits. Don't like oysters? Yerseke is also the centre of the Dutch mussel trade!

324 LIMBURG PIE

DE BISSCHOPSMOLEN
Stenenbrug 3
Maastricht
Limburg
+31 (0)43 327 06 13
bisschopsmolen.nl

Wherever you go in Limburg, you can order coffee and pie. The Bisschopsmolen in Maastricht claims it's the first baker in the Netherlands to only use spelt flour for its pies. Whether this is the secret to their lovely pies, who knows, but we have sampled their gooseberry and cherry pies and they are worth the detour. Next to the bakery, which is housed in a monumental water mill, you can also eat at the restaurant, which serves pies, sandwiches and other cereal products, from their own oven.

325 FRISIAN SUGAR BREAD

BAKKERIJ KEUNING

Merk 15
Workum
Friesland
+31 (0)515 54 12 08
bakkerijkeuning.nl

Frisian sugar bread: it's sticky, not too dry and full of crunchy bits of sugar. Most bakers in Friesland sell this regional speciality. This small bakery in Workum was established about 100 years ago and is now run by the third generation of family bakers.

326 SAUSAGE ROLLS

DIKKE MIK

Halstraat 3
Breda
North Brabant
+31 (0)76 521 63 09
dikkemik.com

A *worstenbroodje* (sausage roll) is not the same as a *saucijzenbroodje*. The latter is made with greasy flaky pastry, whereas the Brabant sausage roll consists of a spicy sausage, made from minced meat, which is wrapped in normal dough. They taste even better when they've just come out of the oven and the soft dough is light brown and crispy on the outside. You can find them in any bakery throughout Brabant. Dikke Mik, on lively Halststraat, in the centre of Breda, is just one baker we recommend.

327 ZEEUWSE BOLUSSEN

BLIEK MEESTERBAKKERS

Damplein 14-16
Middelburg
Zeeland
+31 (0)118 62 84 69
bliekmeester bakkers.nl

Another sticky delicacy, made from white sugar, cinnamon and syrup and rolled into what essentially resembles a poo, the nickname of this Zeeland coffee roll. The bolus was invented in the 16th century, when Sephardic Jews fled Spain and Portugal, settling in Zeeland where they introduced the bola. The bakers of Bliek have been tweaking their recipe for several decades already.

328 FARM CHEESE

KAASBOERDERIJ
DE GRAAF
Buitenkerk 56
Bodegraven
South Holland
+31 (0)172 61 47 04
kaasboerderij
degraaf.nl

Farm cheese or *boerenkaas* is a European protected product, which is made from the raw, unprocessed milk, of cows, sheep or other animals on your own farm. There are plenty of cheese farms in the green heart of the Randstad. The De Graaf family in Bodengraven have been producing their own cheese for just shy of 100 years, which is sold in a well-stocked farm shop.

329 JENEVER

RUTTE
Vriesestraat 130
Dordrecht
South Holland
+31 (0)78 613 44 67
rutte.com

Jenever, which is traditionally a popular spirit in the Low Countries, comes in a young and old variant, depending on the amount of malt wine that was added. Young *jenever* was first created during World War II, when food was scarce. It's usually paired with a beer. The shop and distillery of Rutte in Dordrecht has barely changed since it first opened in 1872. You can now taste young and old *jenever* in the tasting room, in the former living room of the distillery's founder Simon Rutte.

329 **RUTTE**

Food with a
VIEW

330 NOK

FORUM GRONINGEN
Nieuwe Markt 1
Groningen
+31 (0)50 211 01 68
nokgroningen.nl

Located in Forum, the too-good-to-miss cultural hub in Groningen that comprises a library, a cinema, a museum for comics and animation, and maker spaces, all connected by Escher-style escalators. NOK is the tenth-floor rooftop bar and restaurant with a panoramic view of the city and the surroundings. On clear days you might even see the sea.

331 LEV. BY MIKE

Badweg 4
Winterswijk
Gelderland
+31 (0)543 76 90 37
levbymike.com

A beach pavilion in the middle of the Achterhoek that serves world-class dishes, and at reasonable prices at that. This is not exactly the kind of restaurant that needs a nice view, but still. The terrace along the natural swimming pool is a really nice place for a meal nonetheless. Chef Mike's mission is to produce his own take on world cuisine with locally sourced ingredients.

332 REM EILAND

Haparanda-
dam 45-2
[West]
Amsterdam
North Holland
+31 (0)20 244 57 94
rem.amsterdam

REM-Eiland is an artificial island that was built in the 1960s in the North Sea to broadcast (illegal) commercial TV programmes. The pirate island was used for less than a year, but was later converted into a governmental monitoring station. The island was eventually demolished and reassembled in Amsterdam's harbour in 2006. It offers spectacular views and some fine dining as well.

333 'T KALKOENTJE

Utrechtse-
straatweg 143
Rhenen
Utrecht
+31 (0)317 61 23 44
kalkoentje.nl

't Kalkoentje is tucked away in a business park, along a provincial road on the border between Utrecht and Gelderland. The lovely, old-fashioned, cosy restaurant is located in a 17th-century farm with a thatched roof and has a terrace with phenomenal views of the Lower Rhine. Famous for its hospitality, luxurious food and amazing wine list.

332 **REM EILAND**

334 WT URBAN KITCHEN

Heuveloord 25-A
Utrecht
+31 (0)30 303 12 16
wturbankitchen.nl

The city is literally at your feet in this old water tower in Rotsoord. Until a few years ago, this was a run-down former industrial district, but now it's a trendy and up-and-coming area. Have dinner or lunch on the ninth or tenth floor. The tenth floor has floor-to-ceiling windows. You can enjoy spectacular 360° views of the city. There is a cafe on the ground floor, with a terrace on the water.

335 PURE C

STRANDHOTEL
Boulevard de Wielingen 49
Cadzand-Bad
Zeeland
+31 (0)117 39 60 36
pure-c.nl

Some people have described the menu that chef Syrco Bakker serves here as pure food porn. He has already earned himself two Michelin stars. The dishes are a delight to behold and the taste is unrivalled. Be prepared to sample some exciting combos, on beautifully dressed plates. The restaurant is located, in the dunes of Cadzand-Bad, a popular seaside resort in Zeeland Flanders. You can enjoy a beautiful view of the dunes while you eat.

334 WT URBAN KITCHEN

Amazing
V E G E T A R I A N *restaurants*

---

336 **DE NIEUWE WINKEL**

Gebroeders van
Limburgplein 7
Nijmegen
Gelderland
+31 (0)24 322 50 93
denieuwewinkel.com

While not strictly vegetarian, De Nieuwe Winkel does excel in what they like to call 'botanical gastronomy'. Plants take centre stage in this two-Michelin starred restaurant that is a collaboration between chef Emile van der Staak and food forest pioneer Wouter van Eck. Not only are the dishes stunning, the restaurant's interior is equally impressive: located in a former orphanage with an open kitchen so you can see the masters at work.

337 **SHIRAK**

Karrenstraat 14
Den Bosch
North Brabant
+31 (0)73 614 54 62
restaurant-shirak.nl

Vegetarians are always interested in trying something different, like Armenian cuisine for example. Dishes with nuts, fruit, eggplant and yoghurt are served with bread. Meat lovers will also find something to their liking here, because this restaurant is not exclusively vegetarian, although they do have a lot of veggie dishes on the menu. Do try some Armenian tea or cognac after your meal.

338 DE KOP VAN 'T LAND

Zeedijk 32
Dordrecht
South Holland
+31 (0)78 630 06 50
kopvanhetland.nl

If you really need a break, then go to De Kop van 't Land, an inn on the outskirts of Biesbosch, which is just a short bike ride from Dordrecht, where you will be well and truly pampered. Surprising flavour combinations, beautifully dressed Michelin-quality dishes, and extremely friendly waiters. Once you've eaten your fill, you can take a nice brisk walk along the dike or spend the night in the inn.

338 DE KOP VAN 'T LAND

339 **BIJ ALBRECHT**

Gagelstraat 6
Eindhoven
North Brabant
+31 (0)40 737 06 38
bijalbrecht.nl

Who says vegan food is boring? Bernadette and Manfred call their restaurant a plant-based food experience and serve all kinds of nourishing dishes, on beautifully dressed plates, in a white interior with an open kitchen. Tasty food with the added bonus of a smaller carbon footprint.

340 **HAGEDIS**

Waldeck
Pyrmontkade 116
The Hague
South Holland
+31 (0)70 364 04 56
restauranthagedis.nl

Hagedis serves vegetarian and organic food in a stately old school building. The restaurant is part of the residential and working community de Grote Pyr and is run by the residents. Order the menu of the day for a surprise or taste their delicious cheese fondue.

Hidden gems serving
DIVERSE CUISINE

---

341 MANDALIN

Kommel 8
Maastricht
Limburg
+31 (0)43 852 69 63
restaurant
mandalin.nl

Dutch cuisine is no longer limited to hodgepodge and meatballs. You can now eat dishes from around the world, thanks to the diverse population of the Netherlands and the input of newcomers. People have said that the food at Mandalin is actually "better than in Turkey itself". Sample Turkish *mezze* (small snacks) and meat, fish and vegetarian dishes, in a welcoming, nice ambience, just a stone's throw from the Vrijthof. The homemade *baklava* is difficult to resist.

342 JASMIJN & IK

Kanaalstraat
219-221
Utrecht
+31 (0)30 293 89 07
jasmijnenik.nl

The kind of hidden local gem, which is always fully booked. You can sample various dishes from modern Asian cuisine in the Lombok neighbourhood (including Thai, Vietnamese and Cantonese). Plenty of vegetarian options and good wine suggestions. Do try their dessert, made from green tea and basil!

343 EETHUIS DAYANG

Prinsestraat 65
The Hague
South Holland
+31 (0)70 364 99 79
eethuisdayang.nl

This cafe adjoins the garden of Noordeinde Palace and is a lively *toko*, with five small tables. Their speciality is fish fillet in a spicy, sour sauce. Dayang has also a full-fledged restaurant at Wagenstraat 92 in Chinatown.

344 BAR BACHRACH

Javaplein 25
[East]
Amsterdam
North Holland
+31 (0)20 354 40 00
barbachrach.nl

The chef of this Israeli street food restaurant, Yaniv Lenga from Tel Aviv, once said in a local newspaper that "people in this part of Europe don't really know what to do with eggplants". Bar Bachrach is a stylish but casual restaurant on the cosy Javaplein. They serve modern Middle Eastern dishes to share – Israeli tapas, you might say. Think Jerusalem bagels with dip, halloumi or merguez sausages, and lots of eggplant prepared different ways: from dips to carpaccio. Plenty of veggie options too.

345 MEI WAH

Leenderweg 86
Eindhoven
North Brabant
+31 (0)40 211 75 57
meiwaheindhoven.nl

Eindhoven wouldn't be the same without Mei Wah. This restaurant opened in 1965 and is now run by the third generation of family cooks. While they do take-away, the food they serve is above and beyond the usual takeaway fare. Here you can enjoy a copious meal, with pure flavours, because they do not use any flavour enhancers. Taste their steamed oysters or their 'Kip Kerkhof' (chicken thighs with ginger and garlic), a dish that is named after one of their loyal customers.

346 WARUNG GARENG

Schiedamse-
weg 40-A
[West]
Rotterdam
South Holland
+31 (0)10 818 37 21
warunggareng.nl

It's always busy at Warung Gareng and once you've tasted their food you'll see why. Their homemade sate sauce with peanuts is delicious and their filling and nourishing *saoto soup* is an excellent lunch or dinner option. They also have a very good *roti* as a main course (also vegetarian).

DE BEYERD

DRINK 🍷

TERRACE
hang-outs

---

347 ZONDAG
NOORDERPLANTSOEN
Kruissingel 1
Groningen
+31 (0)50 312 35 37
zondagnoorder
plantsoen.nl

The Noorderplantsoen city park is situated in the centre of Groningen. In 1930, they built a stylish pavilion here, which is a mix of the Amsterdam School and the De Stijl architectural style, with large windows that look out onto the pond. It's open all day, from breakfast till dinner, for a cup of coffee or something stronger.

348 DISTILLERY
'T NIEUWE DIEP
Flevopark 13
[East]
Amsterdam
North Holland
+31 (0)6 27 07 60 65
nwediep.nl

Find this small distillery, with its lovely terrace near the orchard and the pond. It is tucked away in Flevopark in the east of Amsterdam in a former pumping station. Here you can sample homemade *jenevers,* made from 100% malt wine, as well as beer or apple cider, with cheese or sausage as a snack.

349 ALOHABAR
BLUECITY
Maasboulevard 102
[East]
Rotterdam
South Holland
+31 (0)10 210 81 70
alohabar.nl

Many people from Rotterdam and the surrounding region still remember BlueCity010, the current 'playground for the circular economy', as the tropical swimming pool it used to be. You can still find a water ride and a water slide here, as well as plenty of unique companies such as Rotterzwam, which grows mushrooms on coffee grounds. Cafe and Restaurant Alohabar has the premium spot, with a huge terrace along the Nieuwe Maas River, near Willemsbrug bridge. A great place for a cup of home-roasted coffee, oyster mushroom *bitterballen* and a drink or a nice dinner.

349 ALOHABAR

350 T-HUIS

350 T-HUIS

John F. Kennedy-laan 15
Breda
North Brabant
+31 (0)76 562 37 80
t-huis.online

The façade of the striking glass T-Huis is decorated with lamp letters, just like Broadway. This place, which has a large terrace, is located in Valkenberg park in Breda. The letters spell the words 'Spaghetti', 'Coffee', 'Sausage' and 'Ice cream'. The building was designed by architect John Körmeling, after the city council redeveloped the park and decided it needed an artwork cum cafe. You can also stop here for a beer or a cheese sandwich by the way.

351 LANDGOED DE WILMERSBERG

Rhododendron-laan 7
De Lutte
Overijssel
+31 (0)541 58 55 55
wilmersberg.nl

From the hillside, you have a view of the country estate that was acquired by a rich textile manufacturer just after World War I. He had a house built here, which is now home to an upmarket restaurant and hotel. You can also stop for a drink after a walk through this lush country estate. The Rhododendron Avenue, which flowers beautifully in May, is one of the better-known attractions of this estate.

352 DE ZEEUWSE HEMEL

Melkmarkt 8
Zierikzee
Zeeland
+31 (0)111 41 70 94
dezeeuwsehemel.nl

Everything in Zierikzee points to the city's rich history. You'll find a cosy garden behind the authentic building called De Zeeuwse Hemel, which was built 400 years ago as an inn. It's a good place for lunch or dinner, made with regional products. They also have a deli and some rooms in the attic and cellar where you can spend the night.

353 DE ZAGERIJ

Rotsoord 7-A
Utrecht
+31 (0)30 400 40 80
dezagerijutrecht.nl

Utrecht has a lot to offer, but it doesn't have much of an industrial heritage. And yet, De Zagerij (the sawmill) with its tall windows, high ceilings and partly original interior points to a history of hard labour. The restaurant has a terrace along Vaartsche Rijn and is located in the former sawmill of the famous Pastoe furniture factory. The factory is living its second life and now houses several small businesses and restaurants.

BREWERIES
to visit

354 DE MOLEN

Overtocht 43
Bodegraven
South Holland
+31 (0)172 61 08 48
brouwerijdemolen.nl

The place to go for anyone who enjoys experimental beers (are you bold enough to sample their Chocolate Raspberry Stout?) although they also serve classics like porter and IPA as well as some very in-your-face barrel-aged beers. The tasting room and beer shop are situated in the old corn mill, while the brewery is just up the road. They organise tours on Saturdays. The Borefts Bier Festival at the end of September is very popular with national and international beer connoisseurs.

355 MAALLUST BREWERY

Hoofdweg 140
Veenhuizen
Drenthe
+31 (0)592 38 89 71
maallust.nl

The Veenhuizen penal colony in Drenthe was also likened to Siberia. It was a self-sufficient penal colony, where 'unadjusted' elements of society lived and work under strict supervision from 1823 onwards. They now brew beer in the Maallust mill, and produce cheese in the adjoining old dairy factory, Kaaslust. You can request a tour of the brewery in the tasting room.

356 SLOT OOSTENDE

Singelstraat 5
Goes
Zeeland
+31 (0)6 14 56 29 81
slotoostende.nl

A city brewery moved into the beautifully restored Oostende Castle, which dates from the 12th century. The brewery, restaurant and hotel are centrally located and have a terrace in a lush garden, attracting a wide audience as a result. They merged with the widely reputed Emelisse brewery, which is known for its barrel-aged beers, among others. Tours through both the brewery and the castle are organised on Saturdays.

357 JOPEN

Gedempte
Voldersgracht 2
Haarlem
North Holland
+31 (0)23 533 41 14
jopenkerk.nl

The Haarlem-based Jopen brewery has been popular with beer lovers for many years. The brewery and grand cafe are located in Jopen church, where you can get an almost intimidating list of beers on tap, which are all produced in-house. The kitchen serves a good burger or a plate of paste, but now and then they also organise special tastings, pairing beer with oysters, chocolate or cheese. Check the events calendar on their website.

358 OEDIPUS

Gedempt
Hamerkanaal 85
[North]
Amsterdam
North Holland
+31 (0)20 244 16 73
oedipus.com

The brewers at Oedipus were inspired by American beer culture. They have a wide array of beers, including their Mannenliefde, a *saison* that won a silver medal at the 2018 World Beer Cup, and their Gaia IPA, as well as some unique seasonal beers. If you like experiments, try the award-winning Gospel, a blend of seven barrel-aged beers. The tasting room in North Amsterdam is very low-key. It has 14 taps – the beers change often – a panoply of bottled beers you can choose from, and a small menu with veggie and non-veggie options.

359 **HERTOG JAN**

Kruisweg 43
Arcen
Limburg
+31 (0)77 473 91 60
hertogjanproeverij.nl

You'd have to be blind not to notice the pipeline, which connects the stark white Hertog Jan brewery with the tasting room on the other side of the road. The pilsner in the tanks is directly connected to the taps as a result. The Hertog Jan pilsner beer is no longer brewed in this photogenic building. Arcen is mainly renowned for its speciality beers. You can tour the brewery or sample the goods on the shadowy terrace, or indoors among the old beer ads and other Hertog Jan paraphernalia. The speciality beers pair nicely with a good, sturdy meal in the cafe.

359 **HERTOG JAN**

Favourite
AUTHENTIC *pubs*

360 **CAFÉ DE BEL**
Gerard Scholten-straat 61-B
[North]
Rotterdam
South Holland

The most convivial cafe in Rotterdam's Oude Noorden neighbourhood is always full, regardless of which weekday you happen to stop by. The patrons in this local watering hole are young and old, the music loud, and the walls are covered with posters, paraphernalia and old guitars. Regular performances.

361 **DE BEYERD**
Boschstraat 26
Breda
North Brabant
+31 (0)76 521 42 65
beyerd.nl

At cafe de Beyerd they already served Belgian beers while the rest of the Netherlands was still drinking Heineken. The cafe is located on the fringe of the centre of Breda. It usually fills up as early as the afternoon and it has all the conviviality of a local pub. They also serve their own De Drie Hoefijzers beer and every dish on the menu of the adjoining restaurant comes with a suggestion for a beer pairing.

362 **CAFÉ DE HETE BRIJ**
Nieuwe Markt 9
Zwolle
Overijssel
+31 (0)38 421 75 26
cafedehetebrij.nl

This cafe in the centre of Zwolle is as cosy as a living room, albeit one with a classic, dark brown wooden interior, with bar stools and walls full of beer ads and other gadgets the owners collected over the years. They have plenty of beers on tap, including their own brews.

363 DERAT

**Lange Smee-
straat 37
Utrecht
+31 (0)30 231 95 13
cafederat.nl**

DeRat grew as Utrecht's city centre became more popular. At the end of the afternoon, the locals arrive, to be replaced in the evening by students and young workers. DeRat has its own special selection of beers, *jenevers,* whiskies and other delicacies that are just slightly different from the usual fare. Check out the framed mummified rat hanging on the wall.

361 **DE BEYERD**

364 DE TIJD

Voorstraat 170
Dordrecht
South Holland
+31 (0)78 613 39 97
detijddordrecht.nl

14 beers on tap which change regularly, and over a hundred bottled beers, a cheese sandwich and a cupboard full of board games: we bet you'll stick around at De Tijd for a while. This cafe is situated on Voorstraat, among antiques shops, bookshops and other interesting shops and has become somewhat of an institution.

365 L'AFFICHE

Jacob van
Lennepstraat 39
[West]
Amsterdam
North Holland
+31 (0)20 612 19 59
cafelaffiche.nl

Café l'Affiche owes its name to the layers and layers of posters that have been pasted on the wall over the years. It's the type of cafe that is becoming increasingly rare in Amsterdam, with a laidback atmosphere, a warm welcome, friendly waitstaff. The terrace gives out onto the canal and faces westwards, meaning summer sun till late in the evening.

366 CAFÉ DE BONTE KOE

Hooglandse-
kerkchoorsteeg 13
Leiden
South Holland
+31 (0)71 514 10 94
cafedebontekoe.net

Everyone is welcome in this tiny but welcoming Leiden cafe (just 36 square metres) including students, businessmen and tourists. The walls are lined with tiled depictions of rural scenes, in the Jugendstil style or the style of the Hague School, which are 100 years old and were installed when this was still a butcher's. The interior hasn't changed much since then.

VINEYARDS
recommended by connoisseurs

---

367 ST. MARTINUS
Rott 21-A
Vijlen
Limburg
+31 (0)43 455 20 27
wijngaard
martinus.nl

The Netherlands is not exactly a wine country. The climate is somewhat cold and humid, something grapes don't really enjoy. Nevertheless, there are now approximately 200 vineyards in the Netherlands and this number is only set to increase due to climate change. One of the oldest vineyards in the Netherlands is situated in the southernmost tip of Limburg. You will feel like a king as you gaze down from the large terrace of the St. Martinus vineyard upon the green, undulating landscape. This 16-acre vineyard, which has already won several awards for its wines, was the first Dutch winery to produce red wines. Now they have a wide selection of wines, including white and rosé. Bergdorpje is a crisp, dry white wine, which you can only find in Vijlen. The vintner Stan Beurskens and his team research techniques to make winemaking more sustainable, as well as grape varieties that are more resistant to fungi, to do away with pesticides altogether. They organise tours Tuesdays through Saturdays, book online. Check out more wineries in the vicinity by following a Route du Vin (more info at *visitzuidlimburg.nl).*

368 BETUWS WIJNDOMEIN

Burensewal 5
Erichem
Gelderland
+31 (0)6 42 10 71 12
betuwswijndomein.nl

This award-winning vineyard in Erichem has a shop, a tasting room and a tour of the vineyard, with an explanation by the vintner Diederik Beker. He has been producing wine here since 2004, in what is one of the larger vineyards of the country. His LingeRood, made from Regent and Pinotin grapes, is aged for 12 months in oak barrels and won an award in 2018. The Betuws Wijndomein also produces fruit juices and a non-alcoholic rosé.

369 DOMEIN HOF TE DIEREN

Arnhemsestraat-
weg 16
Dieren
Gelderland
+31 (0)6 22 39 96 42
domeinhoftedieren.nl

Youp Cretier worked as a financial consultant until he decided to start a vineyard, together with his wife Riet, in 2004. As you enter Hof te Dieren, you will feel as if you have been transported to France. The terrace has a view of the vines, and the cottage garden, where you can also see the pigs foraging. The shop sells wine, as well as products from the garden (jam, preserved courgettes, liqueurs and sausage). Cretier now produces approximately 10.000 bottles of organic wine a year. His Cuvée Willem II is definitely worth trying. The vineyard is beautifully located, and adjoins the Hof te Dieren estate.

370 WIJNHOEVE DE KLEINE SCHORRE

Zuiddijk 4
Dreischor
Zeeland
+31 (0)111 40 15 50
dekleineschorre.nl

This is one of the larger vineyards (10 hectares) in the Netherlands, near the Dreischor ring village. They selected Alsace grape varieties like Pinot Gris, Pinot Blanc, Rivaner and Auxerrois because they pair beautifully with Zeeland specialities like mussels, Oosterschelde lobster, oysters, marsh samphire and sea lavender. Take a tour at De Kleine Schorre, stock up in the shop and enjoy a nice meal and some wine in the tasting room in an 18th-century barn. Good to know: you can spend the night on the campsite.

371 WIJNGOED THORN

Bogenstraat 12-A
Thorn
Limburg
+31 (0)475 56 10 02
wijngoed-thorn.nl

A map of the KNMI, the Dutch meteorological institute, proves that Thorn has the least rain in all the country. Add the Maas gravel and the clay in the soil to this equation and you have all the prerequisites for some tasty wine grapes. The wine from the Belgian-Dutch Maas Valley was protected as a European regional product in 2017. Thorn's Pinot Gris also won an international award.
The tasting room and shop in the 'white village' of Thorn is open Thursday, Friday and Saturday from 2 pm to 4 pm.

Dedicated
COFFEE ROASTERS

372 MAN MET BRIL KOFFIE
Vijverhofstraat 70
[North]
Rotterdam
South Holland
+31 (0)10 307 28 55
manmetbrilkoffie.nl

You can find Man Met Bril coffee in more and more cafes in Rotterdam but the best place to drink it is still among the grinders, the roasters and the hessian bags full of coffee beans in the Hofbogen, with a sweet treat, while you read the newspaper. Man Met Bril has won several awards for its coffees. A 'coffee hotel' (together with a roaster, coffee bar and restaurant) is due to open in 2023.

373 WHITE LABEL COFFEE
Jan Evertsenstr. 136
[West]
Amsterdam
North Holland
+31 (0)20 737 13 59
whitelabelcoffee.nl

The undisputed coffee hang-out of the De Baarsjes neighbourhood, since 2014. The owners Francesco and Elmer prepare one of the best flat whites in Amsterdam. Sit down in one of the many lounge corners on different levels, enjoy some people watching from their tiny terrace or take some beans home with you.

374 VAN ROSSUM'S KOFFIE
Turfstraat 10
Zutphen
Gelderland
+31 (0)6 16 90 69 77
vanrossumskoffie.nl

In addition to espressos, cappuccinos and cortados, Van Rossum also serves different types of filter coffee. Jelle van Rossum sources beans from Colombian, Ethiopian and Congolese growers after which he roasts them himself. It's a great place to while away the time with a newspaper at the reading table or with a book from the adjoining Van Someren & Ten Bosch bookshop.

375 LOCALS

Heuvelstraat 128
Tilburg
North Brabant
+31 (0)13 211 72 61
locals-tilburg.nl

Locals serves everything but on good days, you cannot but notice the scent of freshly roasted coffee. A cosy place for a filter coffee, a simple ristretto or a Vanilla Sky (with vanilla syrup, whipped cream and chocolate shavings)... or why not try an alcoholic coffee-based cocktail?

376 BREW2CUP

Kortestraat 28
Arnhem
Gelderland
+31 (0)26 382 78 99
brew2cup.nl

The owners Cynthia and Erwin bring out the natural flavours of the coffee beans and even succeed in making rabid coffee haters change their minds with their brews. Hide out downstairs in the cosy coffee cocoon with soft chairs and a comfy sofa.

375 **LOCALS**

HARLINGEN LIGHTHOUSE

SLEEP 🌙

UNUSUAL
places to spend the night

---

377 DE KLEINE ANTONIUS
Borgweg 32
Zeerijp
Groningen
+31 (0)6 24 64 82 25
dekleineantonius.nl

Lay your head down to rest on the church organ in this beautiful Baptist church from 1904. The church can also be rented for performances or events, but you'll have it all to yourself if you decide to spend the night here. So play a little ditty on the piano or cosy up to the wood stove. The owner Dick Stukkien has plenty of stories to share about this special place.

378 HORTUS HERMITAGE
Kerklaan 34
Haren
Groningen
+31 (0)50 537 00 53
hortusharen.nl/
hortus-hermitage

Spending the night in an old food silo is always a unique experience, but this one is made even more special because of its location in a botanic garden. The silo's interior is decorated with furniture, made from materials that were gathered in the Hortus and include a desktop made of plant cards. The Hermitage is a retreat. You can stay here for two nights or more, from May till October. According to a romantic, 18th-century custom, hermits were given permission to sleep in the botanic garden, as they were regarded as symbols of the reflective man who is close to nature. And now you can follow in their footsteps.

379 ALIBI HOSTEL LEEUWARDEN

Blokhuisplein 40
Leeuwarden
Friesland
+31 (0)6 12 07 74 49
alibihostel.nl

Many prisons have often been likened to hotels, because of the luxurious conditions in which the prisoners were held. Now that more and more jails are closing their doors, some are being converted into hotels. You can spend the night in the Blokhuispoort, in a sparsely furnished dormitory, or share a bunk bed in one of the cells. For more luxurious accommodation, book a double room with an ensuite bathroom. If your cell feels too claustrophobic, then head to one of the common rooms where you can cook, read a book or have a beer.

378 HORTUS HERMITAGE

379 ALIBI HOSTEL LEEUWARDEN

380 **WINDKETEL**

Watertoren-
plein 8-C
[West]
Amsterdam
North Holland
windketel.nl

This tiny octagonal house near a large white water tower is situated in the Netherlands' first sustainable 'ecodistrict', which is also car-free. It also happens to be near the opular Westerpark. The Windketel project was set up by ten locals, who manage the hotel apartment. The house has a modern look and feel, with Dutch Design furniture, and can be booked for stays of three or more nights.

381 **COCONDO**

Kleinzand 6
Hoek van Holland
South Holland
+31 (0)6 412 494 32
cocondo.nl

Local entrepreneur, bunker aficionado and former photographer Peter de Krom transformed this former WWII-bunker in the dunes with a great eye for detail and a high standard of style and comfort. Lots of original details found their way into the modern and stylish interior. It sleeps two adults and two children, and has a lovely little patio. Profits are reinvested into maintaining and developing cultural heritage and nature.

Rooms with a
BREATHTAKING *view*

---

382 **SWEETS HOTEL**

VARIOUS LOCATIONS
Amsterdam
North Holland
+31 (0)20 740 10 10
sweetshotel.
amsterdam

This unique hotel runs 28 bridge master's houses in Amsterdam. In 2018, they added the one at Amstelschutssluis to their offering. You can only get to this house and lock by boat. While the view from your hotel room is always different, you are definitely guaranteed to have the best view of Amsterdam's canals from your private residence.

383 **STERRENKUBUS**

Dorpsstraat 7
Lattrop-
Breklenkamp
Overijssel
+31 (0)541 22 13 92
sterrenkubus.nl

These cubes all have a transparent roof so it seems as if you are sleeping under the stars. You can see the stars even better with the telescope in your room. The ten cubes – recyclable tiny houses – are just six kilometres from Ootmarsum, next to a centuries-old Saxon farm, where the Rerink family raises Deep Red cattle and likes to share their good life with guests.

384 **SEINPOSTSTELLING**

Seinpostweg 35
IJmuiden
North Holland
+31 (0)6 23 27 42 71
seinpoststelling.nl

Watch cruise ships and fishing boats sail past and enjoy a stunning view of the port, the beach and the pier of IJmuiden from your double hammock. This colourful 40-square-metres apartment is situated in the former signal post at IJmuiden, which is the gateway to the Port of Amsterdam.

385 HARLINGEN LIGHTHOUSE

Havenweg 1
Harlingen
Friesland
+31 (0)6 13 34 43 13
vuurtoren-
harlingen.nl

The lighthouse in Harlingen port is a great starting point for your visit to the Wadden Islands of Vlieland and Terschelling and has been converted into a hotel room. The light at the top, just below the copper dome, has now been replaced with a table for two with a 360-degree view. The lighthouse keeper drops off a basket with breakfast goodies in the morning. There is no lift in the lighthouse!

384 SEINPOSTSTELLING

Sleeping with your
FEET IN THE WATER

386 VILLA AUGUSTUS FLOATING PONTOON

Oranjelaan 7
Dordrecht
South Holland
+31 (0)78 639 31 11
villa-augustus.nl/
hotel

These eight hotel rooms are situated at the rear of Villa Augustus, in a former floating office of the Eerland tugboat service, which was built in 1905. It was moored in the port of Rotterdam as a mobile office for several years. Inside you can see photos of the pontoon's original moorings in Rotterdam's Waalhaven. Villa Augustus has a hotel, a restaurant, a gallery space, a shop and a fantastic cottage garden and orangerie, where they regularly host concerts.

387 WIKKELBOAT ROTTERDAM

Rijnhaven
[South]
Wijnhaven
[Centre]
Rotterdam
South Holland
+31 (0)88 888 70 00
wikkelboat.nl

Sleep in a cardboard tiny house on the water in beautiful Rijnhaven with his historic quays or amid the high-rises of Wijnhaven, in between the Nieuwe Maas River and the Markthal. This floating sustainable wooden houses are wrapped in 24 layers of cardboard and are waterproof thanks to the intermediate Gore-Tex layer. The Wikkelboats have all the mod cons such as a projector, a barbecue and a hammock and some even come with a private jacuzzi.

388 OPOE SIENTJE MUSEUM BOAT

Lindenberg-
haven 1-C
Nijmegen
Gelderland
+31 (0)6 13 11 61 84
opoesientje.nl

Cosy up to the fireplace in the hold. On sunny days, there's always the terrace of course. This boat is moored in Nijmegen's Museum Port, under Waalbrug and near Ooijpolder. It has nine cosy rooms where you can spend the night, such as the 1001night room or the more classic captain's hut, where you get to sleep among the former captain's possessions.

389 KAMPEERVLOT

Marnemoende
Utrecht
+31 (0)167 50 26 21
camping-raft.com

How about taking a canoe trip across the Hollandse IJssel and waking up with a view of the water, in tranquil natural surroundings? This is back to basics camping. You receive your camping equipment on the spot (such as a gas burner, a jerrycan with water, mats to sleep on and a toilet bucket). All you need to bring is your sleeping bag, a pillow, a towel and some food and drinks. In addition to Marnemoende there is also a floating campsite in De Wissen in Limburg and one in De Heen in North Brabant.

390 DE PIER SUITES

Strandweg 150-154
The Hague
South Holland
+31 (0)6 10 72 04 38
piersuites.nl

Scheveningen's Pier was abandoned and neglected for many years, but in 2015, the tide turned. New restaurants and pubs opened here. It's a great place for zip-lining or bungee jumping and what's more, it has several hotel rooms with fantastic panoramic views of the sea from their own terrace.

391 DRIJFPALEIS

391 DRIJFPALEIS

Boterdijk 13
Arnhem
Gelderland
+31 (0)6 10 70 27 96
drijfpaleis.nl

Drijfpaleis is a little like Villa Villekulla, albeit on the water, in Arnhem. The owner Ruud Hilbrands built this houseboat himself, creating his own take on an Italianate style. It has plenty of charm and the ambience is excellent. Choose from two colourful bohemian chic rooms, which come with two house cats and a terrace garden with plenty of mosaics. Good to know: Ruud serves a great breakfast. The boat is within walking distance of the city centre. Open in the summer season.

392 BUYTENPLAETS SUYDERSEE

Badweg 1
Lelystad
Flevoland
+31 (0)320 25 82 53
buytenplaets-
suydersee.nl

There are two tree huts in the oak trees of Buytenplaets Suydersee, a campsite to the east of Lelystad near Markermeer. One is decorated as a hotel suite, while the other is more basic. They both offer fantastic views and have their own terrace. If you're up for something even more unique than a tree house, why not sleep in a sewage pipe or in a tent (a large hammock) in between the trees?

INDEX

COLOPHON

EDITING *and* COMPOSING — Saskia Naafs and Guido van Eijck

GRAPHIC DESIGN — Joke Gossé and doublebill.design

PHOTOGRAPHY — Roel Hendrickx (roelh.zenfolio.com) —
p. 239 Joram Van Holen — p. 250 © T-Huis

COVER IMAGE — Bathing Pavilion in Domburg (secret 13)

PHOTO DE PONT — p. 64 — credits:
Grapes (2010), Ai Weiwei, collection De Pont Museum, Tilburg (NL)
Maar wie ik ben gaat niemand wat aan (1991), Marlene Dumas,
long-term loan by GGz Breburg

The addresses in this book have been selected after thorough independent
research by the authors, in collaboration with Luster Publishing. The selection
is solely based on personal evaluation of the business by the authors. Nothing
in this book was published in exchange for payment or benefits of any kind.

D/2023/12.005/3
ISBN 978 94 6058 3353
NUR 511, 510

© 2019 Luster, Antwerp
Third edition, January 2023 – Second reprint, January 2023
lusterpublishing.com – THE500HIDDENSECRETS.COM
info@lusterpublishing.com

Printed in Italy by Printer Trento.